HISTORY MAKERS

DEVOTIONS, DOWNLOADS & DAD JOKES

Matt Prater

Ark House Press
arkhousepress.com

Some names and identifying details have been changed to protect the privacy of individuals.

Cataloguing in Publication Data:
Title: History Makers: Devotions, Downloads & Dad Jokes
ISBN: 978-0-6456366-1-1 (pbk)
Subjects: Devotional; Christian Living; Faith;

Design by initiateagency.com

In Matt Prater's newest book, you will take a stroll with a shepherd and be treated to a glimpse of his life and musings. He is a collector of scriptural wisdom, life adages and truth. This can only come from a devotion to God and His Word. Matt exemplifies the pastor as described in Ecclesiastes 12:11 - "The words of wise men are like goads, and masters of these collections are like well-driven nails; they are given by one Shepherd."

Dr. Wayne Cordeiro
New Hope Church & College

"I have never met anyone who works harder in serving the Lord than Matt Prater. Matt's secret, I believe, is in his close walk with his Master. In his book he is sharing with us these precious devotional thoughts. I know they will be such a blessing to you. We all need to be constantly hearing the Shepherd's voice."

Bill Newman
Evangelist

"Spending time with God is essential for those who are followers of the way. Matt Prater's devotional reading plan, along with the other chapters of his inspirational book, are written for these times. The practical, down to earth wisdom in this book is written by one of Australia's giants of the faith."

James Condon
Commissioner Emeritus
Salvation Army Australia

I love how this book begins with some beautiful daily devotions on our duty to help the poor and oppressed. In simple and encouraging words, the reader is gently led to reflect and pray. Throughout these pages the reader will not only be drawn to God's Word, but gain insight through Matt's rich life experiences. Read and be blessed!

Cindy McGarvie
National Director
Youth For Christ

This is a book full of quality snacks of truth - easy to digest, sweet to taste, nourishing to the soul and spirit. I was blessed from reading it.

Martyn Iles,
Managing Director,
Australian Christian Lobby

I'm constantly inspired by Matt's love for the Lord, and passion for people, and this oozes out in these pages. But, be warned! I wouldn't suggest you read this devotional - unless you want your heart challenged and maybe even your trajectory changed… the next three months could be the start of something BIG!

Andrew 'Robbo' Robinson
Vision Christian Radio

Matt Prater has worked in Radio since the age of 15, working as an announcer, in sales, training staff and copywriting. He's also worked as a Spruiker, a DJ, & a Children's entertainer. Matt has previously served as a Youth Pastor at Coffs Baptist Church & Coffs C3 Church. More than anything he is passionate about sharing his faith with people on the streets, with business people, students, churches and anyone who'll listen. Over the years he's ministered in over 15 nations sharing the gospel.

Matt is married to Carol and has 3 children, Lydia, Josh and Grace, and they have 2 labradoodles, Tilly & Shiloh. He hosts Weekends on Vision Christian Radio, and has a weekly syndicated show called History makers which airs on over 25 Community stations. Matt is an Evangelist, cleverly disguised as the Senior Pastor of New Hope Brisbane, a great church reaching out to people all over Brisbane. New Hope has a Soup kitchen every Friday morning, and they send out teams to visit over 30 Boarding houses & homeless shelters with food & the gospel. Many have come to Christ through this mission! They are always looking for volunteers & donations! You can also find Matt on Facebook, Instagram, Youtube, LinkedIn, Tik Tok, Spotify, Soundcloud, and Apple Podcasts.

www.historymakersradio.com
www.newhopebrisbane.com
www.historymakersoutreach.com
www.newhopecare.org.au

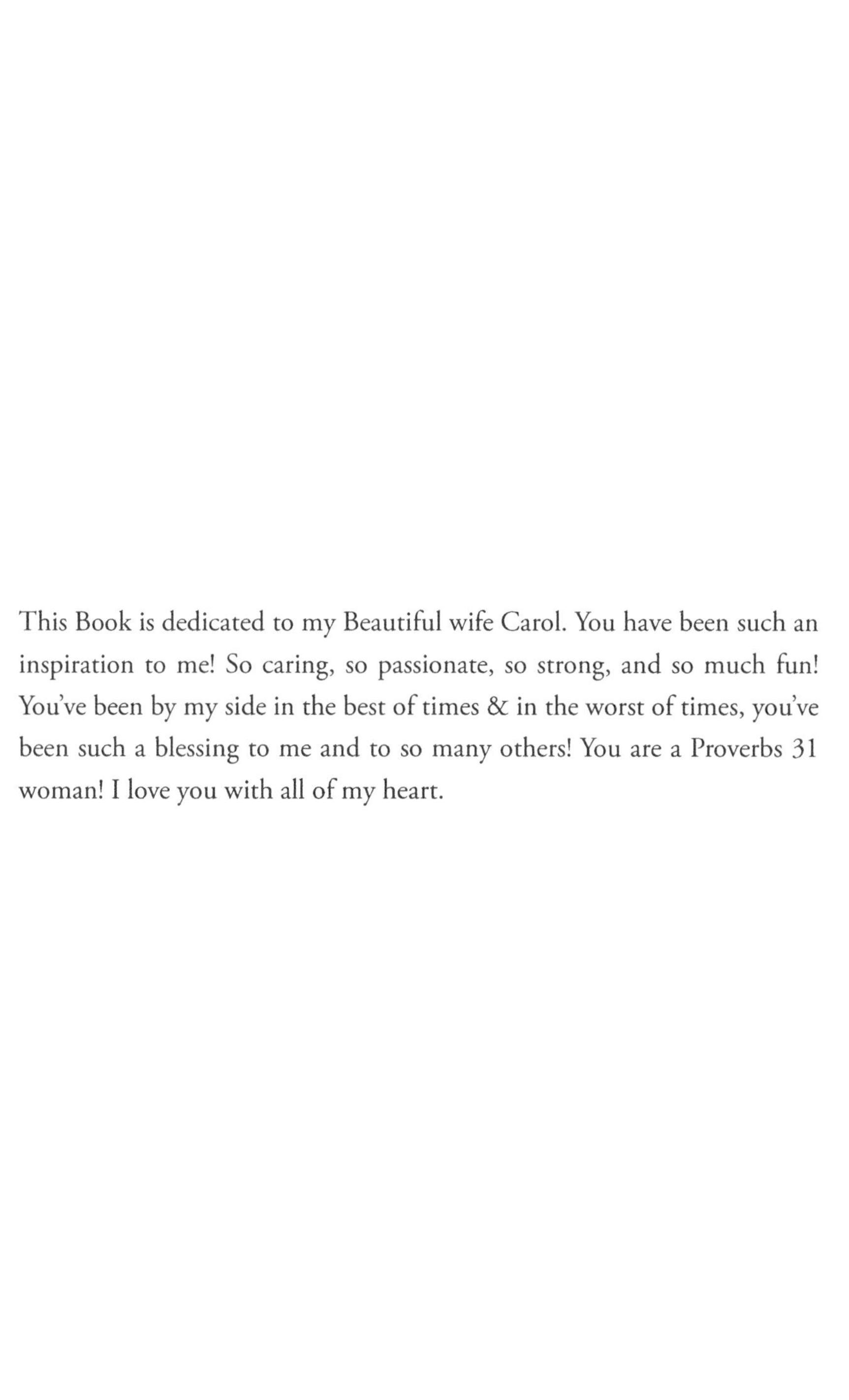

This Book is dedicated to my Beautiful wife Carol. You have been such an inspiration to me! So caring, so passionate, so strong, and so much fun! You've been by my side in the best of times & in the worst of times, you've been such a blessing to me and to so many others! You are a Proverbs 31 woman! I love you with all of my heart.

DEVOTIONALS

When I came to Christ at a youth camp at the age of 15, I remember learning to have a "Quiet time" with God every day. I would read different scriptures, and different devotionals, and pray as the Holy Spirit would lead me. When I became a Pastor, I started the Life Journal reading plan from Pastor Wayne Cordeiro. It changed my life! I've been following this reading plan for many years now. If you want to follow this devotional pattern, here's the explanation:

As we read God's words, we begin to see how God responds to things. Doing daily devotions re-patterns the way we think and transforms the spirit of the mind. Then when we face similar situations as Jesus did, we begin to respond in the same way.

Journaling is an excellent way to both record and process what God has spoken to us. It's also a useful tool to use at a later time, to reflect on and review some of the 'gems' that you have received. Without writing them down, you may forget those blessings and some very important lessons! And while journaling is a very personal time with the Lord, you may want to share some of your daily journaling with your small group or mentors. Through discussion, you may be able to look deeper into what God is speaking to you, gain new insight and even encourage others.

S – for Scripture

Open your Bible to the reading found under today's date of your Bible bookmark. Take time reading and allow God to speak to you. When you are done, look for a verse that particularly spoke to you that day, and write it in your journal.

O – for Observation

What do you think God is saying to you in this scripture? Ask the Holy Spirit to teach you and reveal Jesus to you. Paraphrase and write this scripture down in your own words, in your journal.

A – for Application

Personalize what you have read, by asking yourself how it applies to your life right now. Perhaps it is instruction, encouragement, revelation of a new promise, or corrections for a particular area of your life. Write how this scripture can apply to you today.

P – for Prayer

This can be as simple as asking God to help you use this scripture, or it may be a greater insight on what He may be revealing to you. Remember, prayer is a two way conversation, so be sure to listen to what God has to say! Now, write it out.

And here are some of my devotions…

 DAY 1 

1 John 3:17-18 NIV

'If anyone has material possessions and sees a brother or sister in need but has no pity on them, how can the love of God be in that person? Dear children, let us not love with words or speech but with actions and in truth.'

In Australia, we are a very blessed nation! Some research shows that we are among some of the richest people on the planet. We all have things that we could donate. Whether it's clothes, food, money, toys, etc. Our family regularly does a clean-out to charity, there's so much extra stuff that we don't use! We are blessed to be a blessing. To be a follower of Jesus, we need to walk the walk, not just talk the talk. This week we will see people in need. Think about how you can care for them? How can you bless them & not just give them a handout, but a hand up? What ways can you really change someone's life?

Prayer

Lord Jesus, give me your heart for the poor. Help me always have a heart of generosity & use me to make a difference in others' lives. In Jesus' name, Amen.

Write your thoughts here, what is God saying to you about this passage?

DAY 2

Luke 14:13-14 NIV

'Then Jesus said to his host . . . "When you give a banquet, invite the poor, the crippled, the lame, the blind, and you will be blessed. Although they cannot repay you, you will be repaid at the resurrection of the righteous."'

The basic message of the Parable of the Great Banquet is that God has opened the door of salvation to the Gentiles. The blessings of the kingdom are available to all who will come to Christ by faith. I also see this parable as a beautiful picture of the Church. We invite the poor, the crippled, the lame the blind etc. Our church culture should be a welcoming culture, a gathering culture, & an inclusive culture. Not cliquey, and inbred, but welcoming to all. And I see it as everyone's job to invite people, not just the Pastors & leaders. Think about who you can invite to the banquet of the kingdom of God?

Prayer

Lord Jesus, lead me to the ones you want me to invite into your kingdom. Help me seek & save the lost just like you did Lord. In Jesus' name, Amen.

Write your thoughts here, what is God saying to you about this passage?

 DAY 3 

Zechariah 7:8-10 NIV

'And the word of the Lord came again to Zechariah: This is what the Lord Almighty said: "Administer true justice; show mercy and compassion to one another. Do not oppress the widow or the fatherless, the foreigner or the poor. Do not plot evil against each other."'

Regardless of our political views, we should all have a hear for true justice, mercy & compassion. The Bible makes mention of especially caring for widows, the fatherless, foreigners & the poor. There are many charities who care for these groups, but we should not leave it up to them to care for them. Think of ways you can care for those you know in these categories. Pray for them, make contact with them, ask them how you can help them, build a relationship with them. Ask yourself, "How would Jesus reach out to these precious souls?"

Prayer

Heavenly Father, forgive me for not being pro-active in caring for these precious souls. Show me how I can love with your love. In Jesus' name, Amen.

Write your thoughts here, what is God saying to you about this passage?

DAY 4

Isaiah 58:6-8 NIV

'Is not this the kind of fasting I have chosen: to loose the chains of injustice and untie the cords of the yoke, to set the oppressed free and break every yoke? Is it not to share your food with the hungry and to provide the poor wanderer with shelter — when you see the naked, to clothe them, and not to turn away from your own flesh and blood? Then your light will break forth like the dawn, and your healing will quickly appear; then your righteousness will go before you, and the glory of the Lord will be your rear guard. Then you will call, and the Lord will answer; you will cry for help, and he will say: Here am I.'

I remember doing work experience when I was 16 at Newtown Mission. I was a Country boy in Sydney, and I was shocked at what I saw among the drug addicts & the downtrodden during that week. I realised how sheltered I'd been, and how important it is for Christians to care for those who are at rock bottom. This is true fasting, to share food, to provide shelter & clothing. Have you considered serving at a Soup Kitchen or a homeless shelter? Do you have margin in your life to be intentional & serve the poor?

Prayer

Heavenly Father, show me where I can serve those who you love. Open the right door for me to be your hands & feet. Use me for your glory Lord. In Jesus name, Amen.

Write your thoughts here, what is God saying to you about this passage?

DAY 5

Isaiah 58:9-11 NIV

'If you do away with the yoke of oppression, with the pointing finger and malicious talk, and if you spend yourselves on behalf of the hungry and satisfy the needs of the oppressed, then your light will rise in the darkness, and your night will become like the noonday. The Lord will guide you always; he will satisfy your needs in a sun-scorched land and will strengthen your frame. You will be like a well-watered garden, like a spring whose waters never fail.'

The Prophet Isaiah became agonizingly aware of God's need for a messenger to the people of Israel, and, despite his own sense of inadequacy, he offered himself for God's service, when he said "Here am I! Send me." He challenged people to stop pointing fingers, to stop malicious talk, to care for the hungry & oppressed. And he shared that if this is done, then the Lord will guide, and will satisfy your needs, and will give strength. This is a spiritual principle. When you refresh others, you will be refreshed. Psalm 103 tells us to "forget not his benefits," think about some times when you've helped someone. How did it make you feel? Does it motivate you to help others?

Prayer

Father God, teach us to speak out for you like the Prophet Isaiah did. Give us the right words to say and help us to bless others with our actions as well. In Jesus Name, Amen.

Write your thoughts here, what is God saying to you about this passage?

DAY 6

Proverbs 31:8-9 NIV

'Speak up for those who cannot speak for themselves, for the rights of all who are destitute. Speak up and judge fairly; defend the rights of the poor and needy.'

We all have a voice. We all have a platform. Whether it be to our family & friends, or on social media, or on a bigger platform, we all have an opportunity to speak out for those who can't speak for themselves. When we look at how God raised up Isaiah, Jeremiah, Esther, Daniel, Paul, and many others to speak out, it reminds us that he can raise up anyone! In our times we've seen Mother Theresa, Martin Luther King, and many other Christian leaders to defend the rights of the poor & the needy. They say that "Evil prospers, when good men do nothing." We can all do something to speak up. Think about what platform God has given you. How can you use that platform to speak up for those who can't speak?

Prayer

Father God, grant me boldness to speak up for those who can't speak. Give me words of wisdom to defend the rights of the poor & needy. In Jesus name, Amen.

Write your thoughts here, what is God saying to you about this passage?

DAY 7

Luke 10:36-37 NIV

‘” Which of these three do you think was a neighbour to the man who fell into the hands of robbers?” The expert in the law replied, “The one who had mercy on him.” Jesus told him, “Go and do likewise.”’

Too many are too busy to stop for the one. Don’t be like the Priest or the Levite. ***Martin Luther King Jr*** *said, “The first question which the priest and the Levite asked was: “If I stop to help this man, what will happen to me?” But the good Samaritan reversed the question: “If I do not stop to help this man, what will happen to him?”* Jesus said we are to go & do likewise. One of the worst things about Christianity is that so many who call themselves Christians just talk the talk, but don’t walk the walk. The Book of James tells us that “Faith without works is dead.” Who do you know that you can go & show mercy to?

Prayer

Lord, forgive me for being too busy. Help me always have margin in my life to stop for the one. Fill my heart with your mercy today. In Jesus name, Amen.

Write your thoughts here, what is God saying to you about this passage?

Day 8

Proverbs 3:27-28 NIV

'Do not withhold good from those to whom it is due, when it is in your power to act. Do not say to your neighbour, "Come back tomorrow and I'll give it to you" - when you already have it with you.'

Psalm 24:1 NIV says, 'The *earth* ***is the*** *LORD's,* and everything in it.' When we get the revelation that everything, we have is God's and we are just stewards of His resources, it changes our perspective of what, when & how we give. John Wesley said, *'One of the principal rules of religion is, to lose no occasion of serving God. And, since he is invisible to our eyes, we are to serve him in our neighbour, which he receives as if done to himself in person, standing visibly before us.'* Let's always be generous, & let's never procrastinate. Who can you bless today?

Prayer

Heavenly Father, thank you for all the good gifts you have given me. Help me be a wise steward of what you've entrusted to me. Use me today for your glory. In Jesus name, Amen.

Write your thoughts here, what is God saying to you about this passage?

DAY 9

Proverbs 11:25 NIV

'A generous person will prosper; whoever refreshes others will be refreshed.'

A boy once said to God, "How much is a million dollars to you?" God said, "Just as much as 1 dollar." He then asked, "How long is a million years to you?" He said, "As long as 1 second." He asked God, "Can I have a million dollars?" God said, "In a second." It's a clever joke, but there is a lot of truth to it! As Christians we need to be ambassadors for God in the world. Matthew 7:11 in the NIV says, '"how much more will your Father in heaven give good gifts to those who ask Him!"' God is generous, let's also be generous. And we will be refreshed! Think of someone who you can do a random act of for generosity for today? Don't just think about it, go & make it happen!

Prayer

Father God, thank you for your Word which shows us of your generosity & kindness. Help me reflect your generosity in every part of my life. In Jesus name, Amen.

Write your thoughts here, what is God saying to you about this passage?

DAY 10

Deuteronomy 15:4-5 NIV

'There need be no poor people among you, for in the land the Lord your God is giving you to possess as your inheritance, he will richly bless you, if only you fully obey the Lord your God and are careful to follow all these commands I am giving you today.'

This verse was for the people of Israel, but it has a lot of truth for us today. If the richest people in the world used their wealth to solve the problem of extreme poverty, we would see a massive change! But we have no control of what they do with their money, but we can make a change in the way we use our wealth. I believe in the principle of tithing & offerings, and that we should give to God first, then always be generous to the poor. I believe that you can't outgive God. He is Jehovah Jireh our provider! Be intentional with your giving, make budget & include giving to the causes that are close to your heart…

Prayer

Heavenly Father, thank you for your abundant blessings. Your word says, "To Whom much is given, much is required." Help me always be a giver, and to give in the right places. In Jesus name, Amen.

Write your thoughts here, what is God saying to you about this passage?

DAY 11

Deuteronomy 15:7-8 NIV

If anyone is poor among your fellow Israelites in any of the towns of the land the Lord your God is giving you, do not be hard-hearted or tight-fisted toward them. Rather, be openhanded and freely lend them whatever they need.

One of my relatives used to discourage me from giving to the poor. He used to say, "Charity begins in the home." He would say that I'd never make a difference in the world, so I might as well get a real job, because being a Pastor wasn't ever going to change anything! I told him the story of the Starfish. Where a boy was throwing starfish back in the ocean, after thousands had been beached. Someone challenged him and said he'd never make a difference. He said, "I did for that one," as he saved one more... Let's not be hardhearted or tight fisted... How can you make a difference today?

Prayer

Father God, help me be openhanded & generous to the poor. If there's any greed or selfishness in me, please set me free from those ways. I want to serve you, as I serve others Lord. In Jesus name, Amen.

Write your thoughts here, what is God saying to you about this passage?

DAY 12

Deuteronomy 15:10-11 NIV

'Give generously to the poor and do so without a grudging heart, then because of this the Lord your God will bless you in all your work and in everything you put your hand to. There will always be poor people in the land. Therefore I command you to be openhanded toward your fellow Israelites who are poor and needy in your land.'

When we give & serve, it all comes back to having the right heart in the way we do it. Mother Teresa said, "*Prayer in action is love, and love in action is service. Try to give unconditionally whatever a person needs in the moment. The point is to do something, however small, and show you care through your actions by giving your time … We are all God's children, so it is important to share His gifts. Do not worry about why problems exist in the world – just respond to people's needs … We feel what we are doing is just a drop in the ocean, but that ocean would be less without that drop.*" Check your heart when it comes to giving & serving, is there anything you need to confess to God about your attitude about giving?

Prayer

Heavenly Father, please search my heart. Rid me of any pride, or selfishness, or hypocrisy. Create in me a clean heart today, Lord. In Jesus name, Amen.

Write your thoughts here, what is God saying to you about this passage?

DAY 13

Matthew 25:35-36 NIV

For I was hungry and you gave me something to eat, I was thirsty and you gave me something to drink, I was a stranger and you invited me in, 36 I needed clothes and you clothed me, I was sick and you looked after me, I was in prison and you came to visit me.'

This is a great practical list for giving: Giving food, drink, inviting strangers, giving clothes, visiting the sick & the imprisoned. Some people say to me, I don't know what God has called me to do. I always say, God has already to spoken to us in his Word. This is a list of what he's commanded all of us to do. He's also commanded us in Matthew 28 to preach the gospel to all creation. These two things go hand in hand. William Booth who started the Salvation Army followed the mission, "Soup, Soap & salvation." What a simple mission! Who can you care for practically today? Don't just care for their physical needs, share the gospel with them as well!

Prayer

Lord Jesus, send me to the poor, give me boldness to not just care for the physical, but the spiritual as well. Give me the right words to say, in Jesus' name, Amen.

Write your thoughts here, what is God saying to you about this passage?

DAY 14

Matthew 25:40 NIV

"'The King will reply, 'Truly I tell you, whatever you did for one of the least of these brothers and sisters of mine, you did for me.'"

This poem has always convicted me:
"I was hungry …
And you formed humanities groups to discuss my hunger.

I was imprisoned …
And you crept off quietly to your church and prayed for my release.

I was naked …
And in your mind you debated the morality of my appearance.

I was sick …
And you knelt and thanked God for your health.

I was homeless …
And you preached to me of the spiritual shelter of the love of God.

I was lonely …
And you left me alone to pray for me.

You seem so holy, so close to God …
But I am still hungry … and lonely … and cold …"

~ author unknown ~

Jesus has called us to go to the Last the least & the Lost. Go & be his hands, his feet & his voice today.

Prayer

Lord Jesus, I give you my hands, my feet, my wallet & my voice. Use me for your glory. In your name, Amen.

Write your thoughts here, what is God saying to you about this passage?

DAY 15

2 Cor 4:4 NIV

"“The god of this age has blinded the minds of unbelievers so that they cannot see the light of the gospel of the glory of Christ, who is the image of God.”'

Everywhere I go I see darkness. In the media, in the schools, in the offices, in the shops. People walk around thinking life is about making money and finding satisfaction in things. Or people who don't have any vision, with no idea of what on earth they are here for. People stumble around in the darkness committing sins without knowing the consequences. As Pascal said trying to fill that God-shaped hole with anything they can.

Blinded. Without sight, without vision, no sense of true direction. They are bumping into walls, tripping over, wounding themselves. How will they hear without a preacher? How will the blindfold come off unless we pray? How can the god of this age be defeated unless we are willing to fast and battle on their behalf? Blind people can still hear, can still feel, can still smell. What sound can we make to get their attention? What emotions can we stir, so they feel again? How can we be the fragrance of Christ?

Should we do it like Billy Graham and have crusades? Or like YWAM and preach on the streets? Even through television and radio, within our own relationships and the people we meet, or from house to house. How do we get them to the Lord?

Prayer

Lord when we reach out to others, we pray that you will break the spirit of deception and take the blindfold off in Jesus' name. Teach us what it is to be prayed up as we reach out. Amen.

Write your thoughts here, what is God saying to you about this passage?

DAY 16

Psalm 64:10 NRSV

'Let the righteous rejoice in the Lord and take refuge in him; let all the upright in heart glory him.'

We need a refuge. A shelter. A place where we will be covered from the storms and cyclones around us. A building built on the Rock, not Sand.

Around me I see immorality, marriage separations, backsliders, deception, business injustice, pride, busyness, sin is at my door. We need to spend time with the Lord, who is our refuge. Without the Lord as our refuge, we can easily buckle under the pressure. We can easily carry these burdens ourselves and feel the weight of it all. We need to laugh at the enemy and rejoice in the Lord and praise him in this storm! Let us intercede and stand in the gap for victory over these sins. Let us fast and pray and seek the face of the Lord and ask him to bless the afflicted.

Prayer

Help me stay upright in heart. Search me oh God and know my ways. Don't let sin grab hold of me. Anoint me, strengthen me, set me free!!! Lord, I praise you. Give me your shepherd's heart. Help me give wise counsel. Stir me up to pray. Help me to keep on praying in the Spirit. Lord pour out your spirit! Bring revival! The Battle is yours Lord!!! Amen.

Write your thoughts here, what is God saying to you about this passage?

DAY 17

Psalm 66:19-20 NIV

'"But God has surely listened and has heard my voice in prayer. Praise be to God, who has not rejected my prayer or withheld his love from me!"'

The psalmist finishes with Praise to God. After talking about his sin, his troubles, prison, and his enemies. He could have finished sounding bitter, not better. He could have whinged and said woe is me and complained that the journey he was on was hard and through God's testing God should have helped him more. He wasn't at a place where he was following God to get something out of him. But he revered God and thanked him for listening to his prayer.

So many people think God is distant. An old man with long grey hair and a beard who shoots lightning rods. Bette Midler said, "God is watching us from a distance." But he is right here, his Spirit is in us and through us and with us. Why is it so often when we pray that we feel like we are asking the clouds to help? Why does it feel like he is so far away? I heard the quote, "If God seems so far away, who moved?"

If I have had a really busy week and I'm out at meetings a lot, my wife will say to me, "I feel like I need to get to know you again." We need quality time to rebuild our relationship. We need to do that with God too. He is jealous for our time. He desires to walk with us, to talk with us and for us to be intimate with him. If we draw near to God, he draws near to us. This isn't a guilt trip, where you need to put in more hours. It's a heart attitude of closeness to our Father. God wants and loves having you around him, all day, and all night. He really looks forward to it.

Prayer

Lord Thank you for giving an ear to my prayers! Thank you for not withholding your love for me. Teach me what it means to pray without doubting, I draw near to you and worship you today, all day!!! Amen.

Write your thoughts here, what is God saying to you about this passage?

____

____

____

____

____

____

____

____

____

DAY 18

2 Cor 12:4 NIV

"'was caught up to paradise and heard inexpressible things, things that no one is permitted to tell."'

It sounds like an LSD flashback. Or like something from a Steven Spielberg movie. It's more amazing than anything we have heard or could imagine. We really don't have any idea what God has in store for those that love him.

We see glimpses of heaven in parts of the bible. I've heard stories of people going to heaven, and we are all interested in hearing their stories, but we're all a little sceptical because it's inexpressible things of which they are talking about. Keith Green the Christian music artist, says that if it took God 6 days to create the earth, and Jesus has been in heaven for 2000 years preparing a place for us, this must be like living in a garbage can compared to heaven (my paraphrase).

They must have been some awesome things that Paul heard and saw. He could have become conceited because of these surpassingly great revelations. But God doesn't like us to get ahead of ourselves, pride comes before a fall and God opposes the proud and gives grace to the humble. He allowed this thorn in the flesh, just to keep Paul real. We don't want to be too heavenly minded to be of no earthly good. I actually prayed a prayer "Lord please humble me!" Everything changed after that.

Prayer

Lord, I hunger for more visions and revelations from you. I can't wait to be home with you. I want to humble myself before you every day.

Write your thoughts here, what is God saying to you about this passage?

DAY 19

Matt 6:28-31 NIV

'"And why do you worry about clothes? See how the lilies of the field grow. They do not labour or spin. Yet I tell you that not even Solomon in all his splendour was dressed like one of these. If that is how God clothes the grass of the field, which is here today and tomorrow is thrown into the fire, will he not much more clothe you - you of little faith?'"

Abundance starts with faith. Faith that God will look after us. He is Jehovah Jireh our provider. Yet we can quite easily slip back into the old ways of worrying. Life isn't about things, it's about God and people. We shouldn't worry about clothes and food and money and houses. God always provides.

Abundance begins in your heart. It begins with faith. God has always given me everything I have needed. My cup overflows with blessing. He provides it all. It is all from him and through him and in him that all good things come. So as his children, why do we need to worry? We don't want the Lord to say to us, "You of little faith." We need to have an ever-increasing faith. Faith that will move mountains. Faith that his mighty power and provision will always come through. Even at the last minute. It's a good idea to not let the devil steal or rob your faith. Don't let the worries of the world infiltrate your mind. Laugh at the attacks, let the joy of the Lord be your strength.

Prayer

Lord, increase my faith. Let me be as bold as a lion! Pour out your blessings, more than I could contain. I choose not to worry, not to fear. Help me to walk in your abundant life. Amen.

Write your thoughts here, what is God saying to you about this passage?

DAY 20

Matthew 8:26 CEV

'"Jesus replied, Why are you so afraid? You certainly don't have much faith." Then he got up and ordered the wind and the waves to calm down. And everything was calm.'

The disciples saw Jesus' miracles all the time. They knew of his power; they were with him all the time. Yet they still lacked faith. They were still afraid.

Jesus slept through the storm, and they woke him up. Jesus was very blunt to them. He really rebuked them. He challenged them about being afraid and lacking in faith. We always have a choice everyday - fear, or faith? Fear is the devil's playground. Faith is the Lord's playground. It's black or white. Life or death. Blessing or cursing. Faith or fear.

Chuck Swindoll once said, "Why is it that we talk like Christians but live like atheists?" Why don't we trust in him more? The disciples showed faith by crying out to Jesus and waking him up and asking him to save them. They were worried they were going to drown. There is no reason to fear when Jesus is in the boat of life with you.

Prayer

Lord Increase my faith! I will praise you in any storm! Give me more boldness to overcome any fear in Jesus' name! Amen.

Write your thoughts here, what is God saying to you about this passage?

DAY 21

Matt 13:57-58 NIV

'And they took offense at him. But Jesus said to them, "A prophet is not without honour except in his own town and in his own home."'

Jesus had been teaching great parables about the sower, the pearl of great price, the hidden treasure. They always had to ask him what his parables meant. The people were swayed very easily. Sometimes they would believe and support, other times they would question, and whine and even call for his blood and cry, "crucify him!"

In some towns great miracles would happen, there was a great following and an air of expectancy. Not his hometown. They just remembered him as the Carpenters son, the kid up the street. They were lacking in faith. It would be similar if we were in ministry, and we went back to see people from our past. They would only remember us for who we were then, not for who we are, or what we are doing now for God.

Prayer

Lord, please increase our faith. Help us to believe and receive your teachings and to recognise and appreciate your servants who are your prophets, teachers, and healers as who they are in Christ, not what they used to be. In Jesus' name – Amen.

Write your thoughts here, what is God saying to you about this passage?

DAY 22

Matthew 15:11 NIV

"'What goes into someone's mouth does not defile them, but what comes out of their mouth, that is what defiles them.'"

Jesus called the crowd to him, He was teaching them not to focus on the traditions of men, not to look at the outward things of man, but the heart. The wrong things that we say make us unclean. We need to guard our mouths. But most of all we need to guard our hearts. We need to protect our hearts, so that evil thoughts, murder, adultery, sexual immorality, theft, false testimony, and slander, don't break in. If you have unforgiveness towards someone, it's like letting them live rent-free in your heart. We need Jesus to fill every nook and cranny of our heart. Not just the comfy bits, every hidden room, every attic, every cellar, every inch.

How many times do we say something and think, it would have been good if I had thought about that before I said it? We need to be quick to listen and slow to speak. Ezekiel says that the Lord will take out a heart of stone and replace it with a heart of flesh.

One night when my son was around 2 years of age, I was trying to reply to an important email, when my wife wanted me to bath him. I said in a minute… he was crying, then screaming, and I was almost finished with my email. My wife snapped at me and said that she would do it, which caused me to yell at her. I was in my own world of selfishness. In these moments, it can feel like there is the need to explode and not be Christ-like. In my heart was anger, I nearly let it out. But I caught myself just in time. Proverbs says that the power of life and death is in the tongue, and a fool that repeats his folly is like a dog returning to its vomit. Let's guard our hearts and our mouths. Let's talk the talk and walk the walk.

Prayer

Lord, please help me to guard my mouth and my heart. I give you all my heart today. Create in me a clean heart O God and renew a right Spirit within me. Restore unto me the joy of my salvation. In Jesus' name, Amen.

Write your thoughts here, what is God saying to you about this passage?

____

____

____

____

____

____

____

____

DAY 23

Ecclesiastes 9:3-4 NIV

'This is the evil in everything that happens under the sun: The same destiny overtakes all. The hearts of men, moreover, are full of evil and there is madness in their hearts while they live, and afterward they join the dead. Anyone who is among the living has hope —even a live dog is better off than a dead lion!'

Third Day's song, "Cry Out To Jesus" says: "*There is **hope** for the helpless; rest for the weary; and love for the broken heart; and there is grace and forgiveness; mercy and healing; he'll meet you wherever you are, Cry out to Jesus...*"

No matter what happens in our life or how bad things get there is always hope. With every breath we need to realize that things can get better. In death, for those without Christ, they have no chance of hope ever again.

Solomon says that our hearts are all wicked. We need to acknowledge that as a part of our salvation. It is so clear when you watch television these days. We need to know that we are filled with madness, sinners from birth, and we need to be born again to be free from that sin.

People should be able to see that hope in the way we live, the way we talk, the way we love our families, the way we do business, the way we do church.

Prayer

Lord, anoint us to share your hope with power. Give us your heart for the lost. Amen.

Write your thoughts here, what is God saying to you about this passage?

DAY 24

2 Chronicles 20:17

'You will not have to fight this battle. Take up your positions; stand firm and see the deliverance the LORD will give you, Judah and Jerusalem. Do not be afraid; do not be discouraged. Go out to face them tomorrow, and the LORD will be with you.'

Jehoshaphat didn't have a chance in the natural, Moab and Ammon had vast armies. But they were stupid enough to attack the Lord's anointed. Jehoshaphat said to the Lord,

'" ...We do not know what to do, but our eyes are on you."' 2 Chron 20:12

So, they did what we are all meant to do under pressure, they worshiped, they sent out the worshipers to the front line and the Spirit of the Lord came upon them. After the Lord ambushed the enemy, the fear of the Lord came upon all the kingdoms of the countries when they heard what the Lord had done!

What a powerful witness. We need to always remember to worship the Lord! Praise routs the devil; worship defeats our enemies. If we could truly see in the supernatural realm what happens when we praise in the natural realm, we would realize it is the Sword of the Spirit and the most powerful weapon we have!

Prayer

Lord, help me to remember to seek you first always. Amen.

Write your thoughts here, what is God saying to you about this passage?

DAY 25

Isaiah 9:6-7 NIV

'For to us a child is born, to us a son is given, and the government will be on his shoulders. And he will be called Wonderful Counselor, Mighty God, Everlasting Father, Prince of Peace. Of the increase of his government and peace there will be no end. He will reign on David's throne and over his kingdom, establishing and upholding it with justice and righteousness from that time on and forever. The zeal of the Lord Almighty will accomplish this.'

This passage from Isaiah is written hundreds or thousands of years before Christ, and it so eloquently describes his life. Jesus came as a child, God could have zapped him down to earth as a 30-year-old and saved him all the trouble of childhood and teenage years, but he wanted his son to be one of us. I can testify that he is a wonderful counsellor, he is mighty, and everlasting, and no-one can bring peace like him.

He will reign forever. Right now, we are in between times, we only see pockets of the kingdom coming on this earth. But Isaiah says here of the increase of his government and peace there will be no end. We are a part of that increase. When we accepted the Lord, we became citizens of his kingdom. I can't wait till the end. However, it happens, it will be the crescendo of history, the earth is in birth pains for his second coming.

Is this life really just a dress rehearsal for the real thing? If it is, then we've got to give it our best shot in living in his kingdom now. Everything we do now is in preparation for eternity. Let's make sure we know the ways of his kingdom, now.

Prayer

Lord, I want to serve you the kingdom way, not the worlds way. Let your kingdom come in me! Amen.

Write your thoughts here, what is God saying to you about this passage?

DAY 26

1 Peter 4:10-11

'Each one should use whatever gift he has received to serve others, faithfully administering God's grace in its various forms. If anyone speaks, he should do it as one speaking the very words of God.'

In their single, 'If We Are The Body', Casting Crowns sing '*But if we are the body, why aren't his arms reaching, why aren't his hands healing, why aren't his words teaching?*'

Those words are a prophetic call to the Body of Christ, obviously questioning the church and asking why we are so dysfunctional. Asking why we aren't doing what Jesus did, why we are caught up in committees, and buildings and structure. When it distracts us from doing the work of Jesus.

1 Peter talks about how we are to use our gifts to serve others, to faithfully administer God's grace in its various forms. What are these forms? Teaching the things he has commanded us, healing the sick, feeding and clothing the poor, showing hospitality, visiting the imprisoned, and the list goes on…

The next scripture then says, If anyone speaks, he should do it as one speaking the very words of God. Wow what a responsibility, to speak as though you are speaking the very words of God. We should think before we speak and ask ourselves 'what would Jesus say' in every situation?'

Prayer

Lord, help me hear from you and speak your words. Whether at church, in a school, in meetings, give me your words and your heart for people. Help me use the gifts of our Spirit. Show me how to serve others with the gifts you have given me. Amen.

Write your thoughts here, what is God saying to you about this passage?

DAY 27

John 4:34-35 MSG

'Jesus said, "The food that keeps me going is that I do the will of the One who sent me, finishing the work he started. As you look around right now, wouldn't you say that in about four months it will be time to harvest? Well, I'm telling you to open your eyes and take a good look at what's right in front of you. These Samaritan fields are ripe. It's harvest time!"'

Jesus was rebuking the disciples for caring about food more than the Samaritan woman. He told them not to miss out on the harvest in front of them. They thought that it would only be the Jews that they would minister to, but Jesus was telling them not to be so closed minded. Maybe our harvest fields are bigger than we can see with our own eyesight? Maybe we need to broaden our perspective and ask God to help us see through his eyes?

We need to want to do the will of the One who is sending us into the harvest fields. We should want to find the harvest and we all need to open our eyes and see where God is leading us.

Where is your harvest? Is it your school, university, workplace, your home, or church? Or even just in the community?

Prayer

Lord, we want to make disciples. Let our food be to do your will. Show us where to sow, water and harvest with you… We don't want to miss any fields. Amen.

Write your thoughts here, what is God saying to you about this passage?

DAY 28

Jeremiah 1:7-10

'But the LORD said to me, "Do not say, 'I am only too young.' You must go to everyone I send you to and say whatever I command you. Do not be afraid of them, for I am with you and will rescue you," declares the LORD. Then the LORD reached out his hand and touched my mouth and said to me, "Now, I have put my words in your mouth. See, today I appoint you over nations and kingdoms to uproot and tear down, to destroy and overthrow, to build and to plant."'

Battered Fish sang a song called "*Fearless*" Which said, "*my God made me fearless, I'm clay nothing but clay, moulded my divine hands.*" We need to be fearless in the things we do for God. If we feel he's called us, he will equip us, he will put the words in our mouth, he will anoint us.

Sometimes when we know we have been called to speak publicly at work, at church, at school, at university, we can feel so nervous, vulnerable, and inept and useless for the task. But then when we pray for God's power to do what he has called us to do, he reminds us that he's called us to be his voice to our work, at church, at school, or at university. He will speak to us like he did to Jeremiah, and then we can do all things through him who strengthens us.

If we could see with our spiritual eyes the number of angels around fighting for us, if we could see how the Holy Spirit is working on people, if we could grasp how powerful God is and how he can bless a situation with his hand, we would never have any fear again!

Prayer

Lord, I want to be bolder in my sharing of the Gospel, in every area of my life, through my words and actions. Holy Spirt, please help me. In Jesus' name. Amen.

Write your thoughts here, what is God saying to you about this passage?

DAY 29

1 John 4:19

'We love because he first loved us. If we say we love God yet hate a brother or sister, we are liars. For if we do not love a fellow believer, whom we have seen, we cannot love God, whom we have not seen. And he has given us this command: Those who love God must also love one another.'

John is very black and white in this letter. This was written near the end of his adventurous life as a disciple, and he wants to get to the point. He says it is God's way or the worlds way, the spirit of truth or the spirit of falsehood, love, or fear. Love a brother and you are loving God or hate a brother and you cannot love God. It is black or white, and the gospel is white.

It is easy to see how people in the world can end up hating people, they have no point of reference to forgive. The world says me first, everything else after that. If we have God first, others second, then ourselves, it is clear we cannot hate. To put others first you cannot hate them because hate is a very selfish emotion. So, what is the reasons for hate? People have sinned against you in some way, jealousy, a disagreement, some run in from the past. We need to be white in our relationships. If this is God's will, his Holy Spirit will always guide us in our relationships, he is a spirit of reconciliation.

Prayer

Lord, help me to always have healthy relationships. I pray that you will speak to me any time I need to reconcile with someone. May our church also be a place of healthy relationships. Amen.

Write your thoughts here, what is God saying to you about this passage?

DAY 30

Daniel 4:37

'"Now I, Nebuchadnezzar, praise and exalt and glorify the King of heaven, because everything he does is right and all his ways are just. And those who walk in pride he is able to humble.'"

Nebuchadnezzar was put in his place. God cared more about his heart than his sanity. He was proud and disobedient, and the Lord moulded him until he became humble. How shameful must it have been for his family and friends. Out in the fields eating grass, his hair grew like feathers and his nails grew like claws.

In modern day society, they would have the men in white coats take him away and putting him on medication, until he was a zombie. But God cared more about his heart than all the things people would have cared about. We would say, how could a loving God care about him, by making him go crazy. But God is the potter, and we are the clay. Who are we to say that God is unfair, or that God doesn't know what he's doing.

God loves to be in relationship with us, and he'll give or take away until we are right with him. He is in the business of character building. Through trials and tribulations, through drought and rain, through sickness and in health, God wants us to be right with him. Not proud, not bitter, not selfish, not greedy, not out of balance. A broken heart and a contrite spirit, he is yet to deny.

Prayer

Lord, I trust in you. I know that you know what you are doing. I want to have the right heart before you in all that I do. Everything you do is right, and all your ways are just. Thank you for moulding me. Come and be my potter, Lord. Amen.

Write your thoughts here, what is God saying to you about this passage?

DAY 31

Luke 9:23-25 MSG

"'Anyone who intends to come with me has to let me lead. You're not in the driver's seat—I am. Don't run from suffering; embrace it. Follow me and I'll show you how. Self-help is no help at all. Self-sacrifice is the way, my way, to finding yourself, your true self. What good would it do to get everything you want and lose you, the real you?'"

Christian singer Paul Colman shared how he keeps on trying to take the wheel off Jesus and steer his own life, and every time he does, he crashes and burns. He had a vision once of himself in the front seat of his car holding a kid's steering wheel that Jesus gave him, so he thought he was really driving.

Carrie Underwood, former American Idol winner released a song called "Jesus Take The Wheel," It was played on the radio all over the world and shot to the top of the country music charts. Obviously, the message resonated with the hearts of people everywhere. As humans, we try to steer our lives in the right direction, but when we do we lose ourselves. The only true way to find ourselves is to lose our life for Jesus. Give him the wheel.

We get so caught up in a hedonistic lifestyle, with a me-focused attitude, that we lose the real person we are meant to be. It's like every materialistic thing that we give ourselves to, we are putting on another mask. And to come to Christ is peeling away each mask like peeling an onion. It has lots of layers, with nothing in the end. That's how we are meant to be. Serving him, letting him guide us and lead us, peeling off each mask until there is no me, and all him.

One of my favourite worship songs from David Ruis titled "Lily of the Valley", has a lyric which is repeated over and over: "*More of you and less of me, and more of you and less of me; And more of you, more of you Jesus...*" Just when you think he's sung it too many times, you get it. It's all about Jesus, not ourselves. As we decrease, he increases. That's how we find who we are meant to be. It's all in the serving, suffering, the self-sacrifice, giving him the wheel.

Prayer

Jesus, take the wheel. Amen.

Write your thoughts here, what is God saying to you about this passage?

____

____

____

____

____

DAY 32

Ezra 6:21 NIV

'So the Israelites who had returned from the exile ate it, together with all who had separated themselves from the unclean practices of their Gentile neighbors in order to seek the LORD, the God of Israel.'

They purified themselves and made themselves clean. They celebrated the dedication of the house of God with joy. The Israelites had separated themselves from the unclean practices of their gentile neighbours in order to seek the Lord.

What does it mean to separate ourselves? Some think it's like the Amish and remove yourself from society. Or the exclusive brethren, who build a building within a building to keep out of the world. But I think it's more to do with time, and morals and lifestyle, than hiding away from the lost. It means separating yourself in a fast occasionally. It means not getting drunk like the world does, not being addicted to the idols of sport and media and money. Not to follow the unclean practices in business and relationships that the world follows.

We need to be constantly seeking the Lord. How much do we do without seeking him? We can't be foolish and stay at home each morning until we hear God tell us what to wear, but we need to be open to his leading for the direction we lead in life. This is why it is good to turn from the worldly way of living. Me focused, money focused, image focused. We need to be God focused and Spirit led. We need to seek him by always asking, Lord, what is your will? How can I serve you?

Prayer

I Love the Rich Mullins Song, "*Sometimes By Step*", that says:"I will seek you in the morning and I will learn to walk in your ways and step by step you'll lead me, and I will follow you all of my days." That's my prayer. Amen.

Write your thoughts here, what is God saying to you about this passage?

___

___

___

___

___

___

___

___

___

___

DAY 33

Mark 11:17 NIV

'And as he taught them, he said, "Is it not written: 'My house will be called a house of prayer for all nations?' But you have made it 'a den of robbers.'"

Jesus quotes from Isaiah 56, because the tax collectors were prostituting the temple. Isaiah 56 talks about keeping the law, and honouring God with a life of integrity. In verse 7, it says 'these I will bring to my holy mountain and give them joy in my house of prayer.'

Three things I see in this: Firstly, are 21st century churches known as houses of prayer? We say prayers at the start and end of meetings, we have scheduled and spontaneous prayer meetings, but do we pray so much so that people would identify churches as a house of prayer? A bakery might be called a house of bread because it revolves around bread, a coffee shop for coffee, but is the church known as a house of prayer? Jesus says it should be.

Secondly, it says for all nations. I do not think it means we are to pray for all nations, but all nations should have houses of prayer.

Thirdly, the passage from Isaiah says, he will give us joy in the house of prayer. Joy is so crucial to our mission in life. Who would want to join us if we were a bunch of sour faces? The Bible talks so much about joy, we need to actively seek the joy of the Lord in our lives, to laugh and dance and smile and be light-hearted. When there is Joy from the Lord, we can climb any mountain before us.

Prayer

Lord, I commit myself to always seeking your face. In Jesus' name – Amen.

Write your thoughts here, what is God saying to you about this passage?

DAY 34

Luke 17:3-4 MSG

'"Be alert. If you see your friend going wrong, correct him. If he responds, forgive him. Even if it's personal against you and repeated seven times through the day, and seven times he says, 'I'm sorry, I won't do it again,' forgive him."'

How important is the concept of forgiveness? It is a constant theme throughout scripture. The world is very good at holding grudges and keeping peoples' sins counting against them. Revenge and spitefulness fills television shows and magazines, as well as the political spectrum. In families, workplaces, on the road, in our neighbourhoods. If there's an issue, we want to win, we want people to pay for their sins.

The great thing about being a Christian, is that when God tells us to do something, he also empowers us. He doesn't just give us a command that is too hard for us. He has sent his wonderful counsellor, the Holy Spirit to help us forgive.

We need to forgive as fast as possible, to deal with things and see healing in relationships quickly. God knows that life is much better if we don't hold grudges, it's like having to carry someone else around rent-free all day, the burden is too heavy.

Prayer

Lord, help me to always have a spirit of forgiveness. Thank you for the times I have been forgiven and the times I have forgiven. Amen.

Write your thoughts here, what is God saying to you about this passage?

DAY 35

Job 42:10-11 NIV

'After Job had prayed for his friends, the LORD restored his fortunes and gave him twice as much as he had before. All his brothers and sisters and everyone who had known him before came and ate with him in his house. They comforted and consoled him over all the trouble the LORD had brought upon him, and each one gave him a piece of silver and a gold ring.'

In the world's eyes it seems as though Job got his groove back because he prospered and was blessed in the latter part of his life. But Job never really lost his groove. His groove was his relationship with God, and no matter what was thrown at him, he stood firm on the Rock.

Sure, it would have been a much better life after the sores and the attacks and having all his family and fortune taken away to then be blessed and to have twice as much as he had before. But he was refined in the fire and was proven to be faithful.

I love the last line in the book that says, he died old, and full of years. That's how we should want to die: full of years. Not with empty wasted years, but full of years. Years full of the stuff that God has called us to do.

Prayer

Lord, help me to keep my eyes on you and not on the things of this world. Thank you for all the wonderful blessings you've given me. Help me do the stuff you've called me to. Amen.

Write your thoughts here, what is God saying to you about this passage?

DAY 36

John 11:43 NIV

'When he had said this, Jesus called in a loud voice, "Lazarus, come out!" The dead man came out, his hands and feet wrapped with strips of linen, and a cloth around his face. Jesus said to them, "Take off the grave clothes and let him go."'

Imagine if you were raised from the dead. What would it be like after being dead for 4 days, then walking out alive. You'd be sore and stiff, you'd stink to high heavens, your eyes would have to adjust to the light, you would probably be confused about what day it is.

In verse 44, Jesus said, "Take off the grave clothes and let him go." How many of us still have the old grave clothes on? How many of us have been born again, but still walk around in the old cloak of sin. Wearing the shirt of doubt, the singlet of cynicism, the jacket of fear, the jeans of greed, the underwear of anger, the boots of stubbornness, the grave clothes of the old man.

2 Corinthians 5:17 says, "Therefore, if anyone is in Christ, the new creation has come: The old has gone the new has come." We need to walk around with a new attitude, a new heart, and a new Spirit. The book of James in chapter 1 in the NIV, says, 'Such a person is double minded and unstable in all they do.' We need a single minded resolve to get rid of the old grave clothes, to repent from our sins and burn those stinky clothes into

oblivion. We need to be so passionate about repenting from our sins that we wear our new clothes with joy! That we dance and sing and rejoice for the old has gone and the new has come!

The book of Isaiah says we are clothed with a cloak of zeal. Zeal means enthusiastic diligence. Often the first thing people notice about you is the clothes you're wearing. Let's let those new clothes be the first thing people see about us.

Prayer

Lord thank you for raising me from the dead and giving me a second chance. I want to live like a man raised from the dead and make the most of all you've given me. Help me live like a new creation every day. Amen.

Write your thoughts here, what is God saying to you about this passage?

____

____

____

____

____

____

DAY 37

Matthew 13:54-58

'Coming to his hometown, he began teaching the people in their synagogue, and they were amazed. "Where did this man get this wisdom and these miraculous powers?" they asked. "Isn't this the carpenter's son? Isn't his mother's name Mary, and aren't his brothers James, Joseph, Simon and Judas? Aren't all his sisters with us? Where then did this man get all these things?" And they took offence at him. But Jesus said to them, "A prophet is not without honor except in his own town and in his own home." And he did not do many miracles there because of their lack of faith.'

John Bevere's bestselling book, "*The Bait of Satan*", talks about how people get so easily offended, and it causes divisions and bitterness. In the same way we catch fish with a bait, the devil baits us with a spirit of offence to divide us.

People are the same now, as they were 2000 years ago. Jesus does some wonderful things in his hometown, and the locals have the tall poppy syndrome, and they take offence at him. Sadly, their offence led to a lack of faith and there weren't many miracles because of this.

In churches today, people easily get distracted with the problems, they complain and whine about things, getting offended at the way things are done, and they lose their focus. The focus needs to be on the Lord, not on people. We need to come to church expectant for God to perform miracles.

We need to have faith that the Lord will build his church, and we need to keep our eyes on him.

Luke 18 verse 8 says, '"However, when the Son of Man comes, will he find faith on the earth?"' In the New Living Translation, in Hebrews chapter 11 verse 1, it says, "Now faith is the substance of things hoped for, the evidence of things not seen." This year I've learnt a lot about faith. Faith for finances, for healing, for wisdom and guidance. Every day my faith grows stronger because God is so faithful to me. I never want to be found lacking in faith. I want to step out in faith whenever I can.

Prayer

Lord, help us to be a people of faith, to stand on your word and your promises. Amen.

Write your thoughts here, what is God saying to you about this passage?

DAY 38

Revelation 5:6-10 MSG

'The moment he took the scroll, the Four Animals and Twenty-four Elders fell down and worshiped the Lamb. Each had a harp and each had a bowl, a gold bowl filled with incense, the prayers of God's holy people. And they sang a new song:

"Worthy! Take the scroll, open its seals.
Slain! Paying in blood, you bought men and women,
Bought them back from all over the earth,
Bought them back for God.
Then you made them a Kingdom, Priests for our God,
Priest-kings to rule over the earth."'

Who says church is boring! This is the most dramatic, mind-blowing creative script ever seen!!! Firstly, how many of us fall down and worship the Lord? We stand and clap, raise our hands and sometimes dance a bit, but this is a dramatic act of passion and humility to fall down and worship!

The Bowl of incense holds the prayers of God's people. We need to recognize that God loves our prayers, he cherishes them and stores them up in a golden bowl filled with incense. Our prayers are far more powerful than we will ever realize.

This passage finishes with Awesome worship, proclaiming the Lamb who was slain for us. We must worship him more. Let us make the next year a year of personal worship to our Saviour.

Prayer

Lord, you are worthy of all honour and praise forever. I will worship you with all my heart forever and ever. Amen.

Write your thoughts here, what is God saying to you about this passage?

DAY 39

Hebrews 5:7-10 MSG

'While he lived on earth, anticipating death, Jesus cried out in pain and wept in sorrow as he offered up priestly prayers to God. Because he honored God, God answered him. Though he was God's Son, he learned trusting-obedience by what he suffered, just as we do. Then, having arrived at the full stature of his maturity and having been announced by God as high priest in the order of Melchizedek, he became the source of eternal salvation to all who believingly obey him."'

We can also learn trusting-obedience through suffering. If everything was always rosy in our lives, many would think we would have no need for God.

There is one particular third world country in South Africa, where the suffering and their needs are so great, that all they can do, is see their need for God, and come to him. However, over here in Australia, people have so much, and they think they don't need God!

The reality is that we are all sinners separated from God, and anyone who thinks they don't need God's salvation everyday of their life is living in darkness, and they don't know the truth. Even Jesus, God's own Son, 'cried out in pain and wept in sorrow as he offered up priestly prayers to God.' Heb 5:7 MSG. Let's make sure suffering and hard times doesn't ruin us, but let it develop our character. Let suffering be our teacher not our backbreaker. Lisa Simpson from the television show 'The Simpsons' said, "*Whatever doesn't kill me only makes me stronger*"

Prayer

Lord, thank you for the pain you went through for our gain. Help me keep my eyes on you, no matter what I go through. I need more of you in my life, come and fill me with your Holy Spirit. Amen.

Write your thoughts here, what is God saying to you about this passage?

DAY 40

Judges 18:5-6 NIV

'Then they said to him, "Please inquire of God to learn whether our journey will be successful." The priest answered them, "Go in peace. Your journey has the LORD's approval."'

In Old Testament times, priests were appointed to speak for God, and many had to go through the priests to get to God. It was the priest's job to inquire of the Lord and speak his revelation to the people.

In the New Testament, the Bible says that Jesus became our great high priest, bringing us to God. And those of us who believe in Him have become a royal priesthood, a holy nation, a people belonging to God. We need to recognize this in the churches of today! The Pastors aren't the only priests - we all are! We are all required to seek the Lord, to speak for him, to be his ambassadors. The focus shouldn't be on the stage, but on the seats. Pastors are called to equip the saints to do the work of the ministry. All Christians are saints, and all are called to do what Jesus did.

Apparently over 75% of pastors don't finish their careers in pastoral ministry. I think this is part of the problem. People put all the pressure on pastors to do the work of the ministry, and they get overburdened. We are called to carry each other's burdens. To share the load, we all need to have a heart to serve in the Church, and in our communities. To do the work of the ministry wherever we see a need. Let's never become weary in doing good, let's keep praying for much fruit.

Prayer

Lord, may we be a healthy Bride. Let there be much fruit. Help us to love one another, as you have loved us. Amen.

Write your thoughts here, what is God saying to you about this passage?

DAY 41

1 Samuel 20:42 NIV

'Jonathan said to David, "Go in peace, for we have sworn friendship with each other in the name of the LORD, saying, 'The LORD is witness between you and me, and between your descendants and my descendants forever.'"'

I once heard someone say at the end of your life you will be able to count your faithful friends on one hand. If you think about who would visit you if you were in hospital, who would come to your funeral, who you could go to if you are struggling with something, who you could go on holidays with. In this fast paced life, we have lost the art of good friendship. The kind of commitment and friendship like David and Jonathon had.

They had been through a lot together, through thick and thin. David loved Jonathon as he loved himself. They wept together, fought alongside each other. They were devoted friends.

We do not see much of that in society today. I think if we want good friends, we need to be a good friend to those around us. To move past small talk about work, weather, and other minor issues. We need to be involved in one another's lives, caring for each other, praying for each other, bearing one another's burdens as God instructs us in His Word.

Prayer

Lord, help me be a good friend to those around me. Give me your heart, your love, and your Spirit. Amen.

Write your thoughts here, what is God saying to you about this passage?

DAY 42

Matthew 16:18-23 MSG

"'Study this story of the farmer planting seed. When anyone hears news of the kingdom and doesn't take it in, it just remains on the surface, and so the Evil One comes along and plucks it right out of that person's heart. This is the seed the farmer scatters on the road. "The seed cast in the gravel—this is the person who hears and instantly responds with enthusiasm. But there is no soil of character, and so when the emotions wear off and some difficulty arrives, there is nothing to show for it. The seed cast in the weeds is the person who hears the kingdom news, but weeds of worry and illusions about getting more and wanting everything under the sun strangle what was heard, and nothing comes of it. The seed cast on good earth is the person who hears and takes in the News, and then produces a harvest beyond his wildest dreams."'

These are our 4 options, we have a choice to make, which one will you choose?

1. Shallow Belief
2. Poor character in troubled times
3. Coveting and worrying
4. Producing a harvest

We all need be the fourth person: To produce a harvest beyond our wildest dreams! To have a solid faith, good character in tough times, and not worrying about materialistic things and the worries of this world.

Bible commentator Matthew Henry, in his commentary of Matthew 13:18-23, writes, "*What distinguished the good ground was fruitfulness. By this true Christians are distinguished from hypocrites. Christ does not say that this good ground has no stones in it, or no thorns; but none that could hinder its fruitfulness. All are not alike; we should aim at the highest, to bring forth most fruit.*"

Prayer

Lord, as I draw closer to you, let there be much fruit. I will keep my eyes fixed on you. Show me today, how I can bear the most fruit for you! Amen.

Write your thoughts here, what is God saying to you about this passage?

____

____

____

____

____

____

____

____

DAY 43

Jeremiah 17:7-10 NIV

'But blessed is the man who trusts in the LORD, whose confidence is in him. He will be like a tree planted by the water that sends out its roots by the stream. It does not fear when heat comes; its leaves are always green. It has no worries in a year of drought and never fails to bear fruit. The heart is deceitful above all things and beyond cure. Who can understand it? I the LORD search the heart and examine the mind, to reward a man according to his conduct, according to what his deeds deserve.'

We live for an audience of One. Too many times throughout life, we try to please people. The problem with this, is that there are too many people to please and you will never keep everyone happy. Everyone has different expectations, agendas, and standards. We will all fail someone at some time…

The Bible tells us to live in harmony and unity with others, to love others and encourage others. However, it never says that we must impress anyone. We need to trust in the Lord, to have our confidence in him. Then we will be like a flourishing tree. With no fear of man, always maturing and growing, then no matter what the circumstances around us, we will prosper.

If we relied on our own heart, we would fall with pride and arrogance and become greedy and deceptive. We will be squeezed in the mould of the world. That's what the world does, they follow their own hearts, but they don't realize that their hearts are deceptive above all things and beyond cure. That's why the world is in such a mess. Psalm 19:14 says, "May these words of my mouth and this mediation of my heart be pleasing in your sight..."

Prayer

Lord, I live for you alone. You are my audience of One. Forgive me for trying to be a people pleaser. I choose to obey you, to obey your call on my life. Search me and get rid of anything that's not from you. Amen.

Write your thoughts here, what is God saying to you about this passage?

____

____

____

____

____

____

____

____

DAY 44

Ephesians 4:29-32 MSG

'Watch the way you talk. Let nothing foul or dirty come out of your mouth. Say only what helps, each word a gift. Do not grieve God. Don't break his heart. His Holy Spirit, moving and breathing in you, is the most intimate part of your life, making you fit for himself. Do not take such a gift for granted. Make a clean break with all cutting, backbiting, profane talk. Be gentle with one another, sensitive. Forgive one another as quickly and thoroughly as God in Christ forgave you.'

If you break down life, it is about 80 years, thousands of various kinds of relationships, work, rest, and play, and lots of eating and sleeping in between. They say that we average about 20,000 words a day. So that would be about 5.84 billion words in a lifetime. Imagine the impact of a person's life if they treated every word they spoke, like they were giving a gift to someone? Now you would have to do it in humility, but what if we chose not to waste any words, but spoke what we felt God wanted us to speak all the time?

James 1:19 NLT says, "…be quick to listen, slow to speak, and slow to get angry." Proverbs 10:19 AMP says, "When there are many words, transgression and offense are unavoidable…" Proverbs 18:21 ESV says, "Death and life are in the power of the tongue..."

The impressive thing in this passage is that "His Holy Spirit, moving and breathing in you, is the most intimate part of your life," He can anoint our mouths and give us the right words for the right situation. We must seek him more, and no grieve Him, but let his words flow freely.

Prayer

Father, anoint my lips. Touch them with a hot coal like you did with the prophet Isaiah. May your words be like a fire shut up in my bones which I cannot keep in, like Jeremiah. May my words honour you. In Jesus name Amen.

Write your thoughts here, what is God saying to you about this passage?

___

___

___

___

___

___

___

___

___

DAY 45

John 6:19-20 MSG

'So Jesus explained himself at length. "'I'm telling you this straight. The Son can't independently do a thing, only what he sees the Father doing. What the Father does, the Son does. The Father loves the Son and includes him in everything he is doing."'

I love the title Son of Man for Jesus. Son of God is used a lot in Christendom, and it makes Jesus a little less relatable, but Son of Man speaks of his humanity. He was 100% God and 100% man at the same time. As the Son of God, he had miraculous powers and words. But as a man he went through all of the same struggles and temptations that all of us go through. WOW! To think that that's how much God loves us, that he would become one of us.

The WWJD craze came through clever marketing several years ago. The answer is clear, Jesus would do what he sees the Father doing. This is the key to our lives. We need to base the actions of our life on the sacred conversations we have with the Father. To do the things the Father is telling us to do.

Prayer

Father, let this day count for you. Whatever you've called me to do, may I honour you. In Jesus Name Amen.

Write your thoughts here, what is God saying to you about this passage?

DAY 46

Rev 8:3-4 NIV

'Another angel, who had a golden censer, came and stood at the altar. He was given much incense to offer, with the prayers of all God's people, on the golden altar in front of the throne. The smoke of the incense, together with the prayers of God's people, went up before God from the angel's hand.'

Prayer is powerful. When we pray demons flee. When we pray, God opens heaven and pours out blessings. When we pray, God changes things, and we change too! God covets our prayers.

Normally I listen to a sermon on the trip into work. Today I just worshipped. I sang to the Lord and prayed and felt his presence. I also felt his pleasure. In the same way my wife longs for my attention, even more so, I feel that the Lord wants me to be intimate with him. That my prayers are like incense to him.

I heard on a Christian channel I like to watch, that our culture is based on Greek philosophy. Where our life is split into different categories. Religion or Faith is the sacred section, and the rest is secular, such as family, work, recreation and so forth. However, the Hebrew thinking is that everything is sacred before God, of which our lives become an offering to God whatever we are doing. For example, Paul was serving God whether he was making tents, in prison, on a mission trip, no matter what he was doing, he still served God. His whole life was sacred before God. This is why the scripture says, in 1 Thessalonians 5:16 "Pray continually."

Prayer

Father, make my life a prayer to you. Amen.

Write your thoughts here, what is God saying to you about this passage?

___

___

___

___

___

___

___

___

___

___

___

DAY 47

Acts 14:8-10 NIV

'In Lystra there sat a man who was lame. He had been that way from birth and had never walked. He listened to Paul as he was speaking. Paul looked directly at him, saw that he had faith to be healed and called out, "Stand up on your feet!" At that, the man jumped up and began to walk.'

Wow, what an amazing miracle. Paul, ***saw*** that he had faith to be healed. He was bold enough to call out and say, "Stand up on your feet!" We need to have that same faith, and to look for others with that same faith. I do not think the man was just sitting there and happened to have the faith, he had just heard the powerful preaching, and the faith rose up within him.

In Matthew 9:28-29 NIV, Jesus asked a blind man a question about his faith, he asked, '"Do you believe that I am able to do this?"' "Yes, Lord," they replied.' Then he touched their eyes and said, "According to your ***faith*** will it be done to you"; and their sight was restored. (Emphasis mine). We need to be a people of faith. If you do a word search on faith on the Bible Gateway website, it comes up 422 times. It is running all through scripture, and it should be running all through our lives.

Whatever we are lacking in life, we need to have faith for. Healing, finances, growth, salvations, provision, employment and so on. Society today is so lacking in faith. We have become so cynical and critical. But faith says, God is in control.

Prayer

Lord, I have faith in you, You are Jehovah Jireh, Our Provider, I will trust in you forever. Amen.

Write your thoughts here, what is God saying to you about this passage?

DAY 48

Genesis 39:21-23 NIV

'But while Joseph was there in the prison, the LORD was with him; he showed him kindness and granted him favour in the eyes of the prison warden. So the warden put Joseph in charge of all those held in the prison, and he was made responsible for all that was done there. The warden paid no attention to anything under Joseph's care, because the LORD was with Joseph and gave him success in whatever he did.' Genesis 39:21-23

One of my favourite worship songs is "Blessed Be Your Name" by Matt Redman. Its words are revised but taken from the book of Job. It says, "You give and take away, you give and take away, but my heart will choose to say, Lord blessed be your name." I visited a church a couple of years ago, where the pastor had chosen to take that line ("You give and take away") out of the song, because he thought it could be seen as negative. He obviously just wanted to preach a gospel that said God Gives... But God also takes away. God knows what he is doing...

Joseph was in a place where God had taken things away, again! First being thrown in a pit, and losing his family, then to be elevated in Potiphar's house. Then to have everything taken away, thrown in jail. The scripture says in Genesis 39:21, 'But while Joseph was there in the prison, the LORD was with him; he showed him kindness and granted him favour in the eyes of the prison warden.'

Even when we've had things taken away, even when we are in the prison, in the pit, in the hospital, in the sickness, in the valley, in the unemployment, in the financial crisis, whatever we're in, The Lord is there. Sometimes God takes away, so that we will become better people. So that through trials and tests, they produce character, and perseverance, and patience, and it's like being refined in the fire.

Prayer

Lord, Thank you for all the times you've given, and thank you for all of the times you've taken away. Lord. I'm yours whatever happens. On Christ the solid Rock I stand; all other ground is sinking sand! Amen.

Write your thoughts here, what is God saying to you about this passage?

DAY 49

Philemon 1:4-7 Berean Study Bible

'Paul, a prisoner of Christ Jesus, and Timothy our brother, To Philemon our beloved fellow worker, to Apphia our sister, to Archippus our fellow soldier, and to the church that meets at your house: Grace and peace to you from God our Father and the Lord Jesus Christ. I always thank my God, remembering you in my prayers, because I hear about your faith in the Lord Jesus and your love for all the saints. I pray that your partnership in the faith may become effective as you fully acknowledge every good thing that is ours in Christ. I take great joy and encouragement in your love, because you, brother, have refreshed the hearts of the saints.'

Philemon and his house church had been such a blessing to Paul that he thanked God for them in his prayers. They obviously had so much faith that word was getting around, people were reporting back to him of the great things happening there. And they had a love for all of the saints, so they weren't the kind of group that says negative things against other churches and claims they've got it all right and everyone else is missing it. They had a love for *all* the saints. Such an important reminder for us.

In verse 6, "I pray that your partnership in the faith may become effective as you fully acknowledge every good thing that is ours in Christ." I believe this is one of the wisest pieces of encouragement in scripture. Firstly, Paul is praying that their partnership will become effective in sharing their faith. So, we need to be reminded to pray for each other to be active in evangelism.

But here's the reward of evangelism: 'as you fully acknowledge every good thing that is ours in Christ.' Most of the problems I see with Christians today is a lack of understanding of the good things we have in Christ. We are ungrateful for his blessings, we get disillusioned, sadly people backslide and fall out of ministry, people get distracted with the things of the world. If you are looking outward to others with the good news, it's pretty hard to look inward and lose focus. Jesus commanded us in Matthew 28 to "Go into all the world… Teaching everything he has commanded us."

Prayer

Lord, keep our love for all the saints, all your church, burning bright! I pray that we will be active in sharing our faith, I pray that we will understand every good thing we have in Christ. Refresh our hearts and let your kingdom come in Brisbane Lord. Amen.

Write your thoughts here, what is God saying to you about this passage?

___

___

___

___

DAY 50

Micah 6:8 NIV

'He has shown you, O mortal, what is good. And what does the LORD require of you? To act justly and to love mercy and to walk humbly with your God.'

Firstly, it says, "He has shown you, O mortal, what is good." Since Adam and Eve, God has shown us what is good. He has showed us how to live, through leaders and prophets and his Word. We all know of the good that we ought to do, sadly many of us don't do the good. That's the problem of sin, where we are disobedient to his promptings to do good. Secondly, it says, "And what does the LORD require of you?" This is a question we must ask ourselves all day long. How can I serve you best Lord? Who are you sending me too? What do you want me to do with my finances? How can I best spend the next hour? What do you require of me?

Whatever we do, he wants us, "To act justly" as Proverbs 11:1 NIV says, "the Lord detests dishonest scales…," He cares about our heart most of all. He wants us to live with integrity, to promote justice wherever we can. And then to Love mercy. I heard a guy recently share about an experience where he was taken to hell. He said that there was no mercy there. In his agony and pain, no-one had a moment of mercy or care towards him. Jesus showed mercy to many, he should be our example.

I love the last line of this verse: 'To walk humbly with your God.' Everyday wherever we go, we are walking. Around the house, at the office, at the shops, walking. This is our call above all. To walk humbly with God, listening to his Holy Spirit, not walking proudly, not walking like we are God's superstar, or his top gun, but walking humbly with Him, this will bear much fruit.

Prayer

Lord, Thank you for setting the example for us. I want to please you above all else. Guide my steps today, Lord. Amen.

Write your thoughts here, what is God saying to you about this passage?

DAY 51

John 2:14-17 NIV

'In the temple courts he found people selling cattle, sheep and doves, and others sitting at tables exchanging money. So he made a whip out of cords, and drove all from the temple courts, both sheep and cattle; he scattered the coins of the money changers and overturned their tables. To those who sold doves he said, "Get these out of here! Stop turning my Father's house into a market!" His disciples remembered that it is written: "Zeal for your house will consume me."'

We need to understand that we are all unique and we display our emotions differently. However, Ephesians 4:26 NIV reminds us, "In your anger, do not sin." There is a line we can cross when we are angry, the Holy Spirit can give us self-control to not cross over that line. In today's Scripture, Jesus had a righteous anger. Zeal for his Father's house had consumed him. He would not let his Father's house be turned into a "den of thieves" as one version puts it.

We in the church need to constantly examine ourselves, that we are honouring the Lord in His House. He said his house is a house of prayer for all nations, that there should be a word of instruction, a revelation etc. That we speak to one another in psalms, hymns, and spiritual songs. That we should not give up the habit of meeting together as some do.

It's interesting too that Jesus cleared out the Jewish temple of worship here, and Paul tells us that our bodies are the Temple of the Holy Spirit. We need to keep our bodies clean in the same way that Jesus cleaned out the Temple in this passage.

Prayer

Lord, I pray that as a church we will honour you in your house. I pray that I will worship you well with my body, I pray that we will get rid of any idols, and worship you only. Come and clean out whatever you need to Lord! Amen.

Write your thoughts here, what is God saying to you about this passage?

DAY 52

Ephesians 2:20-22 MSG

'God is building a home. He's using us all—irrespective of how we got here—in what he is building. He used the apostles and prophets for the foundation. Now he's using you, fitting you in brick by brick, stone by stone, with Christ Jesus as the cornerstone that holds all the parts together. We see it taking shape day after day—a holy temple built by God, all of us built into it, a temple in which God is quite at home.'

I saw a house on the television recently. It toppled over a cliff because it was built on a shaky foundation. All the hard work and planning, all the excavating, the cleaning, the painting, the renovations, whatever it was used for, all gone, because of one simple oversight: Shaky foundations.

I see too many people without a firm foundation in life. We fall into 3 categories, and we choose which category we are in. 1. No foundation at all, these people blow through life with no firm beliefs and values, and no purpose. 2. A shaky foundation, they profess to follow Christ, but live a life of hypocrisy and they just talk the talk, but don't walk the walk. "having a form of godliness but denying its power." (2 Timothy 3:5) 3. A strong foundation. Like the Apostles and Prophets, these are the overcomers, the ones who when trouble comes, they run to God, not away from God. They are active in the ministry God has called them too, they know the Word and live the Word. They are the ones like Peter who Jesus said in Matthew 16:18 in the NLT, "upon this rock I will build my church, and all the powers of hell will not conquer it." Jesus builds his Church through the overcomers.

I believe the local church is the hope of the world. God is using us to bring his kingdom on the earth. We need to keep letting him build us. He is our Cornerstone, he is our Rock, he is our refuge.

Prayer

Lord, I commit to being an overcomer for you. Amen.

Write your thoughts here, what is God saying to you about this passage?

DAY 53

Ephesians 3:20-21 NIV

'Now to him who is able to do immeasurably more than all we ask or imagine, according to his power that is at work within us, to him be glory in the church and in Christ Jesus throughout all generations, for ever and ever! Amen.'

When racehorses race, all they see is a narrow view in front of them. They have been fed well, trained, and exercised, groomed for victory, but all he can see is the racetrack before him, or another horse behind him. How many of us live like that? We just live life in the same old routine, and all we have is a small short-term vision…

God is able to do immeasurably more than all we ask or imagine!!! It is God that saves souls, it's God that provides finances, it's God that provides real estate, it's God that releases people for ministry, it's God that parted the Red Sea, it's God that knocked down the walls of Jericho, it's God that raises the dead and heals the sick.

I think sometimes God likes to put us in a place where we will fail unless a miracle comes through. He likes to stretch our faith, so it will grow like a muscle.

Prayer

Lord, you have always been a faithful Father to me. I choose to be a faithful son to you. Here am I, send me. I pray that you will pour out more blessings than we could only imagine!!! We praise you for the rain, and we ask for spiritual rain to come down on us too, Lord, Amen.

Write your thoughts here, what is God saying to you about this passage?

Day 54

Philippians 2:14-16 NIV

'Do everything without grumbling or arguing, so that you may become blameless and pure, "children of God without fault in a warped and crooked generation. Then you will shine among them like stars in the sky as you hold firmly to the word of life. And then I will be able to boast on the day of Christ that I did not run or labor in vain.'

I have heard that if you dig a hole deep enough, that even though it's broad daylight you can see the stars above. Interesting that the stars are still shining up there, but we just can't see them because the sun is so bright.

Stars are an amazing contrast to the dark night. Paul is using this example here that people are crooked and depraved, and as Christians we are called to shine in this dark and evil world by doing everything without complaining or arguing.

Clearly from this scripture it is a sin to complain or argue. We need to be realistic if there are issues choose the right way to deal with them, but sadly we often deal with things the wrong way.

Prayer

Lord, I choose to honour you with my words and actions. Help me keep my eyes on you and not problems. Amen.

Write your thoughts here, what is God saying to you about this passage?

DAY 55

Philippians 3:3

'The real believers are the ones the Spirit of God leads to work away at this ministry, filling the air with Christ's praise as we do it. We could not carry this off by our own efforts, and we know it—even though we can list what many might think are impressive credentials.'

We need to be led by the Holy Spirit. How do we know if someone is led by the Holy Spirit? They bear the fruit. We need to give ourselves that checklist every day! Love, joy, peace, kindness, gentleness, faithfulness, goodness, and self-control. If people do not notice that in our actions, words, and hearts, then we are doing something horribly wrong.

If we are not doing things by the Holy Spirit's leading then we are building in vain. It is interesting that so many people class fruit as numbers and finances and buildings etc. God's real growth is in your heart, your character, your temperament, your attitude.

Are we filling the air with God's praise? Do we pray unceasingly? This is the call. Everyday our fruit of the Spirit quota and praising God quota should be increasing, for if we are staying at the same level, we are backsliding! We are not meant to be doing things with our own credentials and our own ways. God's ways are higher than our ways. It is infinitely and eternally more important to be led by the Spirit and have the right heart than any amount of human success.

Prayer

Lord, help me to worship you through praising you and praying without ceasing and allowing the Holy Spirit to show us how to increase our fruit every day. Amen.

Write your thoughts here, what is God saying to you about this passage?

DAY 56

1 Timothy 3:8-12 MSG

'The same goes for those who want to be servants in the church: serious, not deceitful, not too free with the bottle, not in it for what they can get out of it. They must be reverent before the mystery of the faith, not using their position to try to run things. Let them prove themselves first. If they show they can do it, take them on. No exceptions are to be made for women—same qualifications: serious, dependable, not sharp-tongued, not overfond of wine. Servants in the church are to be committed to their spouses, attentive to their own children, and diligent in looking after their own affairs. Those who do this servant work will come to be highly respected, a real credit to this Jesus-faith.'

The Bible is full of check lists. I like to call them 'Heart check lists.' These can be, 'The Ten Commandments, the fruits of the Spirit, The Beatitudes, guidelines for church leaders and leaders in the community and so on. A lot of these lists cover ways that we should live, but the outward fruit of our lives, comes from our inward workings, from our heart. Proverbs 4:23 in the New Heart English Bible says: 'Guard your heart with all diligence, for out of it is the wellspring of life.' We need to keep scrubbing our hearts, check them regularly, ask those who we are accountable to, "How is my heart?"

The Word of God is the best way to check your heart, Heb 4:12 in the NIV says, 'For the word of God is alive and active. Sharper than any double-edged sword, it penetrates even to dividing soul and spirit, joints, and marrow; it judges the thoughts and attitudes of the heart.' If someone is falling in sin, losing their temper, causing trouble, gossiping, stirring up dissension, or whatever kind of sin, it's an outward fruit from their inward uncleanliness.

That's why I love King David's heartfelt cry in Psalm 51 ASV so much. He cries out: 'Create in me a clean heart, O God; And renew a right spirit within me.'

Prayer

Lord, I give you, my heart. Clean it out and 'renew a right Spirit within me.' Amen.

Write your thoughts here, what is God saying to you about this passage?

DAY 57

Jonah 3:1-2 MSG

'Next, God spoke to Jonah a second time: "Up on your feet and on your way to the big city of Nineveh! Preach to them. They're in a bad way and I can't ignore it any longer." This time Jonah started off straight for Nineveh, obeying God's orders to the letter.'

How many times do we do a Jonah? We run away from our calling, or we get distracted from our core mission, or we procrastinate and put off what we feel called to do. It has been said, that if the devil can't kill us, he'll at least try to make us so busy that we are distracted and can't achieve what we have been called to.

It is interesting in The Message translation, in Jonah 3:3, it says, "This time Jonah started off straight for Nineveh, obeying God's orders to the letter." We need to learn from our mistakes. We need to constantly re-evaluate and debrief and improve what we are doing. It is like the saying, 'If we do what we've always done, we'll get what we've always got.'

The question we need to always ask the Lord is this: "How can I serve you best today, Lord?" Even if it is 8:00 at night and we feel like we've wasted our day doing other things. Is it a phone call we need to make, or an email he wants us to send, or to bless a member of the family. We need to obey God's orders to the letter. The Bible says to make the most of every opportunity. It also says whatever you put your hand to, do it with all your might.

Prayer

Lord, though at times I might feel like Jonah, like wanting to run, or be apathetic with my call, or to be average at what I am doing. I commit to you to rise up and answer your call on my life. Lord, what do you want me to do today? Amen.

Write your thoughts here, what is God saying to you about this passage?

DAY 58

2 Timothy 3:16

'All Scripture is God-breathed and is useful for teaching, rebuking, correcting and training in righteousness, so that the servant of God may be thoroughly equipped for every good work.'

When Paul wrote this, he was talking about our Old Testament scriptures. He probably didn't even know that this letter of instruction was going to be included in the Canon of scripture one day.

The Hebrew word for breath is Ruach. The breath of God was on Paul as he was writing this, as with Moses and David and all the 40 writers of scripture. We need the same Ruach in our life. God breathing on our words, our emails and in our families, as well as in our hearts. You can't feel or smell someone's breath unless you're close to them. This requires intimacy, an element of trust. It's hard for us to let people invade our personal bubble. But that's what our Father requires. He longs and yearns for us to stop being so busy and to obey Ps. 46:10 "Be still and know that I am God" (NIV). To listen to his still small voice.

He wants to teach us, and rebuke us, and correct us and train us in righteousness, so that we may be thoroughly equipped for every good work. He loves us too much to leave us the way we are. He has a vision for us, he knows our potential and wants us to grow into it. He does this by breathing his Ruach on us.

Prayer

Breathe on me breath oh breath of God. Amen.

Write your thoughts here, what is God saying to you about this passage?

DAY 59

Mark 13:32-37

'But about that day or hour no one knows, not even the angels in heaven, nor the Son, but only the Father. Be on guard! Be alert! You do not know when that time will come. It's like a man going away: He leaves his house and puts his servants in charge, each with his assigned task, and tells the one at the door to keep watch. Therefore keep watch because you do not know when the owner of the house will come back—whether in the evening, or at midnight, or when the rooster crows, or at dawn. If he comes suddenly, do not let him find you sleeping. What I say to you, I say to everyone: 'Watch!'

Jesus is coming back soon. For some reason, he chose us to be living in these exciting last days, he chose us to run anchor in the relay race. The anchor is the one with the most responsibility to bring it home, to make sure we finish well.

Most Christians don't even think about the return of Christ. This whole chapter in Mark warns us to be awake, to be prepared, to ready ourselves for the end of days.

Every day, there are people we encounter, who need love, people who need someone to pray with, lost people who need to be saved, sick people who need to be healed. Sadly, many of us are sleeping. Jesus commands us to watch, to be on our guard, to be alert, not to be deceived. I don't want to be found sleeping. I want to be found wide awake, doing everything I can for the return of our king. To say I've run the race, I've finished well.

Prayer

Lord, revive me, anoint me to be awake and alert for you. Show me each day, how I can serve you better. Give me the right words to say. Amen.

Write your thoughts here, what is God saying to you about this passage?

DAY 60

Galatians 5:22 MSG

'But what happens when we live God's way? He brings gifts into our lives, much the same way that fruit appears in an orchard—things like affection for others, exuberance about life, serenity. We develop a willingness to stick with things, a sense of compassion in the heart, and a conviction that a basic holiness permeates things and people. We find ourselves involved in loyal commitments, not needing to force our way in life, able to marshal and direct our energies wisely.'

They say that in the first few moments people meet you, they make a judgement about you. They check out the clothes you wear, the look on your face, the way you are standing, and they put you in a box. They say, "This person is rich," or "this person is depressed" or "Wow I like what I see."

After spending time with someone you get to see the fruit of their lives. Jesus said in Matthew 7:20, NIV 'Thus by their fruit you will recognize them.' So if you want to know what a person is really like, not just from outward appearances, look at the fruit of their lives. This passage shows the fruit of the Holy Spirit in someone's life. They have affection for others, exuberance about life and serenity. We develop a willingness to stick with things, a sense of compassion in the heart, and a conviction that a basic holiness permeates things and people. We find ourselves involved in loyal commitments, not needing to force our way in life, able to marshal and direct our energies wisely.

I love various kinds of fruit, but I also love being around people with good spiritual fruit. It's tasty it's refreshing, It's like being given a great gift to be around someone with good fruit.

Prayer

Holy Spirit, I pray that you will fill me and lead me, help me bear the fruit that brings glory to the Father and blesses those around me. Amen.

Write your thoughts here, what is God saying to you about this passage?

DAY 61

1 Cor 12:25-26 MSG

'The way God designed our bodies is a model for understanding our lives together as a church: every part dependent on every other part, the parts we mention and the parts we don't, the parts we see and the parts we don't. If one part hurts, every other part is involved in the hurt, and in the healing. If one part flourishes, every other part enters into the exuberance.'

1 Corinthians 12 is one of the most thumbed through sections of my Bible. I have always been fascinated by Paul's teaching on Spiritual Gifts, and the lack of correct usage in the Churches. Not just the lack of correct usage, but the lack of usage all together! I think Paul puts this section in the middle of his teaching on spiritual gifts because we need to acknowledge that we are in this thing together! We all function in different gifts at various times, but too many of us don't use our gifts that the Lord has given us. Spiritual Gifts are for edification. Our edification and of the body. We all need edification and strengthening. If any of us in the church aren't functioning in the gifts we are meant to, then the body of Christ won't function as it is meant to. When I did a great spiritual gifts test, it helped me see where my strengths are and to focus in those areas.

I love this passage of Scripture because it shows how we are a community, a family. Close enough to know that if one of us is struggling, we will know it. Not a bunch of pew sitters who don't know each other, but friends, brothers, and sisters. "If one part hurts, every other part participates in the hurt, and in the healing. If one part flourishes, every other part enters into the exuberance"

We need to be a part of the church with our eyes wide open. Being involved in the lives of those around us. Encouraging those who are struggling, spurring one another on towards love and good deeds. Seeing the gifts in people and fanning the gifts into flame.

Prayer

Lord show me what it is to eagerly want spiritual gifts. Help me be an encourager to those in the body of Christ around me. Amen.

Write your thoughts here, what is God saying to you about this passage?

DAY 62

Matthew 27:50-53 MSG

'But Jesus, again crying out loudly, breathed his last. At that moment, the Temple curtain was ripped in two, top to bottom. There was an earthquake, and rocks were split in pieces. What's more, tombs were opened up, and many bodies of believers asleep in their graves were raised. (After Jesus' resurrection, they left the tombs, entered the holy city, and appeared to many.)'

That one moment split time in half, from BC to AD. From the old covenant to the new covenant. From the law of sin and death to the law of the Spirit of life. From the need for animal sacrifices to atone for sin, to the ultimate sacrifice. No more thick curtain in the temple, between the people and God. We can now come boldly to the throne of grace with direct access through Christ. It wasn't a man ripping the curtain from bottom to top, but God ripping it from top to bottom. I've heard grace described as 'God stooping down to us.' God stooped down and tore the curtain in two, the final nail in the coffin to religion.

Jesus was the man who spoke vehemently against the Pharisees and the Sadducees and the religious scholars who could quote the scriptures chapter and verse, but their hearts were far away from God. The man who called the temple courts a den of thieves and made a scene tearing down the tables of the moneychangers.

Jesus died to break the curse of that shallow religion and usher in a new way of coming to God. Worshiping him in Spirit and truth. Having the law written on our hearts and not on tablets of stone. And he didn't leave us alone to try in our own strength to work it all out. He gave us his precious Holy Spirit, the wonderful Counsellor, who guides us into all truth.

Prayer

Thankyou Lord for the sacrifice you made. You laid down your life for me, I lay down my life for you, Lord. Amen.

Write your thoughts here, what is God saying to you about this passage?

____

____

____

____

____

____

____

____

DAY 63

Psalm 138:2-3 NIV

'I will bow down toward your holy temple and will praise your name for your unfailing love and your faithfulness, for you have so exalted your solemn decree that it surpasses your fame. When I called, you answered me; you greatly emboldened me.'

Boldness is a particularly important quality for a Christian. Here David is calling out to God, and God made him bold and stout-hearted. David had a lot of important decisions to be made. He had a lot of opposition, a kingdom to oversee, too many wives and concubines and battles to fight. He would have had so many decisions to make and so many advisors telling him what to do.

What does he do? He calls out to the Lord; he writes Psalms and commits his way to his Father and God's word. Proverbs 28:1 ESV says 'The wicked flee when no one pursues, but the righteous are as bold as a lion.' James 1:8 KJV says 'a double-minded man *is* unstable in all his ways.'

We need the same boldness that God gave David. Boldness to make wise decisions, boldness when we pray for people, boldness when we are under attack, boldness when we preach and proclaim the good news. Not a false boldness, full of pride and selfish ambition, wielding authority like an arrogant business tycoon, but a boldness rooted in the humility we have before God. Because all we do is for him and through Him and with Him.

Prayer

Father, I humble myself before you and ask for your boldness in all I do. May I bring glory to you today. Amen.

Write your thoughts here, what is God saying to you about this passage?

Day 64

Acts 5:3-5

'Then Peter said, "Ananias, how is it that Satan has so filled your heart that you have lied to the Holy Spirit and have kept for yourself some of the money you received for the land? Didn't it belong to you before it was sold? And after it was sold, wasn't the money at your disposal? What made you think of doing such a thing? You have not lied to men but to God."'

With great revival comes great holiness. In the book of Acts there is awesome revival! Thousands saved, healed, delivered, people giving money to the Lord, lots of awesome things happening, and God is not letting anyone get away with their lies. Ananias and Sapphira both fell dead on the spot for lying to God about their giving. In Malachi 3:9, God's people are under a curse because they are robbing him of his tithes and offerings.

God requires much of us. When he moves powerfully, there is a price to pay. He wants us to be fully devoted in mind body, soul, spirit, time, house, and wallet. If you take a look at someone's bank statements, you can see who they worship, by the places where they put their money. Some of us need to get born-again in our wallet too!

John Ortberg preached at the Willow Creek Summit about how we need to confess and turn from our shadow mission, so we can get on with God's mission for our lives. He confessed that his shadow mission is "Man's approval" Once he had dealt with that and confessed it to his fellow leaders, he could overcome it and move on with God! Here Ananias and Sapphira had a shadow mission of greed, and financial gain. God dealt with it severely, he demands holiness from us. The Bible says, “be perfect as our heavenly Father is perfect.” It is a high standard, but with the power of the Holy Spirit, “All things are possible for him who believes.”

Prayer

Lord, I lay any shadow mission down at your feet, and ask you to empower me to overcome it, and walk in holiness before you. In Jesus name, Amen.

Write your thoughts here, what is God saying to you about this passage?

____

____

____

____

____

____

____

____

DAY 65

Acts 26:12-16 MSG

"'One day on my way to Damascus, armed as always with papers from the high priests authorizing my action, right in the middle of the day a blaze of light, light outshining the sun, poured out of the sky on me and my companions. Oh, King, it was so bright! We fell flat on our faces. Then I heard a voice in Hebrew: 'Saul, Saul, why are you out to get me? Why do you insist on going against the grain?' "I said, 'Who are you, Master?' The voice answered, 'I am Jesus, the One you're hunting down like an animal. But now, up on your feet—I have a job for you. I've handpicked you to be a servant and witness to what's happened today, and to what I am going to show you."'

I remember doing woodwork at school. They showed us how you can go with the grain of the wood or against it. Going against it is harder and messier and just doesn't feel right. Here in the Message translation, God says, "Why do you insist on going against the grain?" to Saul. This is God – Yahweh, Jehovah. The Ancient of days, speaking audibly to this Christian killer. Wow!! God is Sovereign. When He wants someone. He gets them!

Here Saul is commissioned to do God's work. To show others who are going against the grain and turn them around. As God continues to say in verses 17-18: "'I'm sending you off to open the eyes of the outsiders so they can see the difference between dark and light, and choose light, see the difference between Satan and God, and choose God. I'm sending you off to present my offer of sins forgiven, and a place in the family, inviting them into the company of those who begin real living by believing in me."

Now nearly 2000 years later, that's what we are also called to do. To open the eyes of outsiders. Like Evangelist Reinhard Bonnke recently said, "Any church that isn't preaching the gospel to the lost, isn't doing its job properly!"

Prayer

Lord, anoint me, like you anointed Paul to open the eyes of outsiders to your Good News. In Jesus name. Amen.

Write your thoughts here, what is God saying to you about this passage?

DAY 66

Psalm 23:5 MSG

'You revive my drooping head; my cup brims with blessing.'

Psalm 23, heard at funerals all over the world, speaks of our God of comfort, our good Shepherd. Time after time, I see people with drooping heads. Like sheep without a Shepherd, wandering… You cannot see where you're going if your head is drooping. Our God is a Reviver! In the New Testament there is a verse that says God's power is at work within us. The word power is the Greek word *energeo*, where we get our word energy.

There have been countless times when I have been exhausted or tired or unwell, and I have to preach or go to a meeting and somehow, by God's Grace, he revives my drooping head.

How would you feel if you went to a restaurant and they filled your cup halfway, whether you look at it as half full or half empty, it's not what you paid for. God fills our cup of life to overflowing.

Prayer

Lord, I am grateful for your blessings. Thank you for always reviving me so my head does not droop! Amen.

Write your thoughts here, what is God saying to you about this passage?

DAY 67

Luke 21:1-4

'As Jesus looked up, he saw the rich putting their gifts into the temple treasury. He also saw a poor widow put in two very small copper coins. "Truly I tell you," he said, "this poor widow has put in more than all the others. All these people gave their gifts out of their wealth; but she out of her poverty put in all she had to live on."'

She put in all she had to live on. She put in more than all the others.

Jesus looks at the woman from a heavenly perspective. It's not the amount you give, but the heart behind the giving. The woman was grateful to God. She wasn't on her own throne, God was. Even though it meant she had no money left. This is the kind of follower that pleases the Lord. Not someone who is rich and being selfish in their giving, but someone who is sold out to giving to God, literally.

If Jesus noticed that woman's heart, then he must notice my heart now when I give. He must see when I give and think, "I better not put in too much this week, got to watch the bank balance." And he must see when I give a lot when I do not have money, and he must be pleased. And I know he blesses me for it! The currency of heaven is completely opposite to the world. In the world it's how much you give that is important. In heaven it's the heart behind what you give that matters the most.

Prayer

Lord, thank you for all you've given me. I pray that I always put your kingdom first with finances. You are Jehovah Jireh my provider, your grace is sufficient for me. Amen.

Write your thoughts here, what is God saying to you about this passage?

DAY 68

Matthew 6:6

'But when you pray, go into your room, close the door and pray to your Father, who is unseen. Then your Father, who sees what is done in secret, will reward you.'

Six times in this chapter Matthew uses the 'R' word (*reward*). In the context of giving, praying, and fasting he says go ahead and do these things. But if it's done with a prideful heart, showing off in front of people, you've already received your reward. It's important to see the message behind the text here. He's asking the question, are you doing these things as a show for others to see? Or are you doing it truly because you have your heart in the right place.

When it comes to the part where we receive the reward, it can be either rewards on Earth, or in heaven. Whether you receive them now or later, you will receive a reward. I love and welcome the rewards here, an abundant life on earth, but it's a great revelation to know you are storing up treasures in heaven. We'll spend a lot more time there, than down here! Jesus has gone to prepare a place for us! I once heard the saying that Christianity has a great life insurance plan. The benefits are eternal, and out of this world!

This chapter is central to our faith. Give, pray, and fast. Just do it for Jesus, don't care who sees, we live for an audience of One.

Prayer

Father, I recommit myself to the basics, like the Apostles in Acts, to prayer and ministry of the Word. I'm grateful for your reward program, it's by far the best one I've joined. Forgive me for being like the pagans and chasing after worldly things. I will seek first your kingdom today! 'For yours is the kingdom, the power and the glory forever and ever.' Amen.

Write your thoughts here, what is God saying to you about this passage?

DAY 69

John 18:36

'Jesus said, "My kingdom is not of this world. If it were, my servants would fight to prevent my arrest by the Jewish leaders. But now my kingdom is from another place."'

Interesting that Jesus made this statement when that's actually what Peter did! He cut off a soldier's ear with his sword to protect Jesus from being captured. Jesus famously said in Matthew 26:52, in the NIV, "for all who draw the sword will die by the sword." At the end of this chapter, Barabbas was freed, and he was a part of an uprising! Jesus could have led a political uprising, he had the numbers of followers, the opportunity was there. But he had to fulfil what his Father had ordained him to do. To bring the Kingdom of God, a spiritual kingdom.

One of the greatest criticisms of "religion" is that it's started wars and caused so much trouble on the earth. Jesus didn't come for a physical overthrow; he came with an unseen kingdom. Whenever there was a miracle, it was the kingdom of light overcoming the kingdom of darkness.

What are the weapons of our kingdom? Prayer, servanthood, giving, love, the word of God. Not guns, or bombs, or cyber warfare. But spiritual weapons to defeat the kingdom of darkness.

Prayer

Lord, give me insight into your kingdom. Help me fix my eyes on the things unseen, not on the things of this world. Give me kingdom eyes, kingdom hands and a kingdom heart. In Jesus name. Amen.

Write your thoughts here, what is God saying to you about this passage?

DAY 70

Jeremiah 31:33-34 MSG

'This is the brand-new covenant that I will make with Israel when the time comes. I will put my law within them—write it on their hearts! —and be their God. And they will be my people. They will no longer go around setting up schools to teach each other about God. They'll know me firsthand, the dull and the bright, the smart and the slow. I'll wipe the slate clean for each of them. I'll forget they ever sinned!" God's Decree.'

It's amazing to look at history, to see the way God and man have developed relationship. Adam and Eve walked with God in the cool of the day. Abraham was a man of faith in God, but was a pagan, he didn't have the law, he just had faith. Then the Law came through Moses, and Israel followed it and was blessed. And when they disobeyed it, they were cursed. Then the promise of a brand-new covenant, comes through the prophet Jeremiah. A brand-new covenant. The law on people's hearts. Through Christ, this is what is available to us. Romans 8:2 ESV says, "For the law of the Spirit of life has set you free in Christ Jesus from the law of sin and death."

I love the last bit, "They'll know me firsthand, the dull and the bright, the smart and the slow." Thankfully, I can still know the Lord, even though I'm dull, and slow! Seriously, it blows my mind to think that people can know God from the CS Lewis' and the Ravi Zacharias' geniuses of the world, to the young children, the uneducated, the intellectually challenged, we can all know him firsthand. I'll only find out in heaven, but I have a hunch that the most educated, may be at a disadvantage. As 1 Corinthians 8:1 says, "knowledge puffs up, but love builds up."

Knowing God is always the most important thing. It's the meaning of life. And anyone can know him. Whatever tribe or tongue, old or young.

Prayer

Thank you, Lord for your new covenant. Through the blood of Christ, we can come boldly before the throne of grace. Thank you for your law in our minds and on our hearts. In Jesus' name Amen.

Write your thoughts here, what is God saying to you about this passage?

____

____

____

____

____

____

____

____

DAY 71

Acts 8:20-23

Peter answered: "May your money perish with you, because you thought you could buy the gift of God with money! You have no part or share in this ministry, because your heart is not right before God. Repent of this wickedness and pray to the Lord in the hope that he may forgive you for having such a thought in your heart. For I see that you are full of bitterness and captive to sin."

How you use money is a great test of the heart. Ananias and Sapphira learned the hard way, dying on the spot when lying about money. Here's Simon's test. He'd been following Phillip for some time, and had been baptised, so he had the elementary teachings of Christ. And he so wanted the power to pray for people and see them baptised with the Holy Spirit, he thought he could simply pay some money.

Peter boldly rebukes him. Using the gift of discernment, he brings to Simon's attention, the condition of his heart. The fact that he "followed" Phillip around, and that he wanted the power, says that he wanted to go further in ministry. Peter effectively steps him down from ministry but gives him a choice in verses 22-23: '"Repent of this wickedness and pray to the Lord in the hope that he may forgive you for having such a thought in your heart. For I see that you are full of bitterness and captive to sin."'

The good news is that Simon received this word, and we can safely assume he continued in ministry. Verse 24 says, 'Then Simon answered, "Pray to the Lord for me so that nothing you have said may happen to me.'" This is the first sign of a repentant heart.

Prayer

I pray that Godly leaders will speak to me so boldly if I ever go off the tracks like that. And I pray for boldness to speak the truth to others like that when it's needed. In Jesus name Amen.

Write your thoughts here, what is God saying to you about this passage?

DAY 72

2 Kings 6:16-17

'"Don't be afraid," the prophet answered. "Those who are with us are more than those who are with them." And Elisha prayed, "Open his eyes, LORD, so that he may see." Then the LORD opened the servant's eyes, and he looked and saw the hills full of horses and chariots of fire all around Elisha.'

How many times in scripture do we see the words, "Don't be afraid." Clearly, fear is one of the enemies most used weapons. The truth is in the natural, the odds are almost always against us. If we walk by sight and not by faith, we will be crippled by fear. But if we allow the Lord to open our supernatural eyes, to see with the eyes of faith, we will always know, "Those who are with us are more than those who are with them." 2 Kings 6:16 NIV

Many times, I have been overwhelmed by the circumstances in the natural. Looking at the financial challenges and thinking, where will the money come from? Looking at the natural and waying up the odds is the worldly way of looking at things. Think of David in front of Goliath, Moses in front of the Red Sea, Jonah before Nineveh, Esther before the king. Repeatedly, people of God had the odds stacked against them. But if God is for us, who can be against us? Greater is he that is in me than he that is in the world. Without Faith, it is impossible to please God.

Prayer

Lord, I fix my eyes on you, open my eyes. Let me see with the eyes of faith, to walk by faith and not by sight, may the words "the Battle is your Lords" always be on my lips! In Jesus name Amen!

Write your thoughts here, what is God saying to you about this passage?

DAY 73

Galatians 6:2 NIV

Carry each other's burdens, and in this way you will fulfill the law of Christ.

What a beautiful picture of the New testament Christian. Before this verse Paul is saying, "if someone is caught in a sin, you who live by the Spirit should restore that person gently." As a Pastor, nothing shocks me anymore. I think I've come across people committing almost every Sin known to man, and I've seen many people restored back to a righteous life, led by the Spirit. I think a key word here is gently. That's how Jesus changed everything. He restored people gently. Like the woman caught in adultery, the Law said to Stone her, the Pharisees called for her death. But Jesus said, "He who is without Sin, cast the first stone. One by one they all dropped their stones and admitted their own guilt. And Jesus said, where are your accusers? You need two or three witnesses to accuse someone of Adultery under the law. Then He says, Go and Sin no more. He restores her gently. Not Greasy Grace, which would be Go and keep doing it and keep asking forgiveness. He firmly, but gently said, go and Sin no more.

We are called to do the same with those who are caught in Sin. When a fish is caught in a net, we could cut it in half, and it would die. Or we could gently untangle it so it can be set free. That's what it means by "You who live by the Spirit." We are called to carry each other's burdens. That's the beauty of church. When you are caught in Sin, whether it be greed, or pride, or bitterness, or sexual sin, or stealing, no matter how bad the sin, we don't condemn, we don't show greasy grace, we gently restore. It breaks my heart when people don't come to church because they're caught in sin and think the roof will cave in! It should be the place where they can be restored, gently. A burdened shared, is a burden halved. This is how we fulfil the Law of Christ. Loving God, Loving people.

Prayer

Father, give me your heart for those caught in sin. Help me to minister to them, as the Holy Spirit leads, with love, patience, and compassion. In Jesus' name – Amen.

Write your thoughts here, what is God saying to you about this passage?

DAY 74

John 18:36 NIV

'Jesus said, "My kingdom is not of this world. If it were, my servants would fight to prevent my arrest by the Jewish leaders. But now my kingdom is from another place."'

Jesus could have led a political uprising; he had the numbers, and the opportunity was there. Instead, he came to bring the Kingdom of God, a spiritual kingdom.

One of the greatest criticisms of "religion" is that it has started wars and caused so much trouble. Jesus didn't come for a physical overthrow; he came with an unseen kingdom. Whenever there was a miracle, it was the kingdom of light overcoming the kingdom of darkness.

The example of some Muslims trying to introduce Sharia law is an example of trying to overthrow a system with a religious system. Jesus had no such plan. His plan was to see people transformed by the Gospel, then that would bring God's rule and reign in people's lives.

What are the weapons of our kingdom? Prayer, servanthood, giving, love and the word of God. Not guns, or bombs, or cyber warfare, but spiritual weapons to defeat the kingdom of darkness.

Prayer

Lord, give me insight into your kingdom. Help me fix my eyes on the things unseen, not on the things of this world. Give me kingdom eyes, kingdom hands and a kingdom heart. In Jesus' name. Amen.

Write your thoughts here, what is God saying to you about this passage?

DAY 75

Mark 8:27-30 NIV

'Jesus and his disciples went on to the villages around Caesarea Philippi. On the way he asked them, "Who do people say I am?" They replied, "Some say John the Baptist; others say Elijah; and still others, one of the prophets." "But what about you?" he asked. "Who do you say I am?" Peter answered, "You are the Messiah." Jesus warned them not to tell anyone about him.'

Most Jews, including Peter, one of the disciples, thought that the Messiah would be a political ruler, and didn't understand that Jesus would be a spiritual king.

In Mark 8, Peter and Jesus are talking. Peter had just said Jesus is the Messiah, a momentous revelation and proclamation. Then when Jesus talked about his death and resurrection, Peter rebuked Jesus, the one whom he had just called messiah!

It then says that Jesus rebuked Peter, but he spoke directly to Satan. In verse 33, we read:

'…"Get behind me, Satan!" … "You do not have in mind the concerns of God, but merely human concerns."'

Was Satan possessing Peter? Was it a deceptive demon, under Satan's commands? Was the Evil Spirit oppressing Peter, not possessing Peter?

It may seem a bit harsh that Jesus rebuked him so bluntly. Jesus clearly didn't have a fear of confrontation. And as the Rabbi, he had the authority and right in that culture to speak so bluntly.

For me, the application is twofold. To speak out boldly against anyone who is speaking out of line like Peter was. To walk in my authority and rebuke Satan whenever he speaks through someone.

I need to remember to be careful when I speak. To be careful not to open my mouth to change feet; not to have my mind merely on human concerns, but the concerns of God.

Prayer

Lord, well done on the way you handled Peter! Give me the gift of discerning of Spirits, and the boldness to rebuke Satan where needed. Help me to always have in mind the concerns of God. I repent from my human concerns, for yours is the kingdom the power and the glory forever. Amen!

Write your thoughts here, what is God saying to you about this passage?

___

___

___

___

DAY 76

Numbers 11:29 NIV

'But Moses replied, "Are you jealous for my sake? I wish that all the LORD's people were prophets and that the LORD would put his Spirit on them!" Then Moses and the elders of Israel returned to the camp.'

Who'd want to be a pastor? All he knows is he's heard from God and he's following the voice of the Lord. The congregation, however, want better food, better directions, better facilities, more in their budget, better car parking, better signage, more teaching on this subject, more ministries for their kids, more, more, more…

It was the same with the Israelites and Moses. There was amazing, supernatural provision of manna from heaven. They were privileged to receive these blessings, yet they were sick of it. They coveted what they had in the good old days of Egypt.

There is something in our fallen fleshly nature that makes us whinge and be ungrateful, just like the Israelites here.

God raised up 70 elders to share the burden, he put the Holy Spirit on them, they were anointed to lead. And here his young protégé, Joshua is worried about a couple of leaders who are prophesying. And Moses, as a true leader says in Numbers 11:29, NIV:

"'Are you jealous for my sake? I wish that all the Lord's people were prophets and that the Lord would put his Spirit on them!'"

What a great leader's heart. Not wanting to control it all and lord it over people, but a releasing heart, a father's heart.

God will lead us. God will provide. We must trust our leaders. Be grateful for what the Lord has given us. Don't covet the old days of Egypt, don't look for greener grass. Water the grass you have been given, sow where you are, and you will reap a harvest. You will bear fruit.

Prayer

Thank you Lord for your Manna in my life! I am grateful. Forgive me for the times I had ever grumbled and wished things were better. We will follow you wherever you lead. You have always been faithful and you always will be! Praise you for the wonderful financial provision in the last couple of days, and for the provision to come! Amen!

Write your thoughts here, what is God saying to you about this passage?

____

____

____

____

DAY 77

Ps. 4:4 NIV

'Tremble and do not sin; when you are on your beds, search your hearts and be silent. Offer the sacrifices of the righteous and trust in the LORD.'

There is a key here about sin. When you sin, you have to pay the consequences. God has already told us what sin is, and The Holy Spirit convicts us when we are tempted to sin. As this Psalm says when we are on our beds we are to search out hearts and be silent. Here David says to offer the sacrifices of the righteous. In the Old Testament that was the rule. In the New Testament we offer ourselves as a living sacrifice. We trust in the Lord.

He says, 'Tremble and do not sin.' This is good advice. To tremble does have negative connotations, but there is a time for everything. God is a God of Love, but we must also tremble before his awesome power and as we fear him, we do not sin.

Prayer

Lord, thank you that in the midst of trouble, you are our firm foundation. On Christ the Solid Rock I stand all other ground is sinking sand. Let the light of your face shine on us. Fill my heart with joy may grain and new wine abound. In peace I will lie down and sleep, for you alone, LORD, make me dwell in safety. Amen.

Write your thoughts here, what is God saying to you about this passage?

DAY 78

Isaiah 14:12-13 NKJV

'How you are fallen from heaven, O Lucifer, son of the morning! How you are cut down to the ground, You who weakened the nations! For you have said in your heart: "I will ascend into heaven, I will exalt my throne above the stars of God;..."'

This verse gives an insight into Satan's fall. He was the son of the morning, implying he was beautiful, like the rising sun. He was cut down. He weakened the nations and he'll exalt his throne above the stars of God. Clearly, his weakness was Pride. A weapon well used in churches today. There have been many great men and women become full of themselves and fall.

James 4:6, NIV, clearly says: 'God opposes the proud, and gives grace to the humble.' Proverbs 16;18, NIV, says: 'Pride goes before destruction, a haughty spirit before a fall.' It's much better for God to humble you than for your own actions to cause you to fall…

2 Chronicles 7:14, NIV, says: 'If my people will humble themselves and pray and turn from their wicked ways…'

We need to guard our hearts, and continually give praise and glory to God. We need to pray the dangerous prayer "Lord Humble me." But only if you are ready for anything!

Prayer

Lord, I give you my heart; I humble myself before you and ask you to mould my heart. In Jesus' name. Amen.

Write your thoughts here, what is God saying to you about this passage?

DAY 79

John 4:53 NIV

'Then the father realized that this was the exact time at which Jesus had said to him, "Your son will live." So he and his whole household believed.'

There is a TV show about a family who all get superpowers, and they are using them for good, to change the world! Interesting that the world loves to watch any entertainment about superpowers, when the Bible is full of people with super natural powers! As Christians, we are called to function in them the way the disciples did!

Jesus' supernatural power healed the boy of his fever, and because of that miracle, the whole family believed!

I revert time and time again to using my own words and strategies to share the Gospel, and God still works, and people get saved. But time and time again, witnessing is coupled with signs and wonder that confirm the preaching of the Word. It's harder to do the Supernatural stuff, but we must step out on faith and be bold, and miracles will come!

Prayer

Lord, Use me to do great exploits in your name, give me more boldness. Use me in this great harvest, Lord. I pray that those in our churches will see their families and friends saved. Let there be more miracles Lord! Amen.

Write your thoughts here, what is God saying to you about this passage?

DAY 80

2 Kings 6:16-17 NIV

'"Don't be afraid", the prophet answered. "Those who are with us are more than those who are with them." And Elisha prayed, "Open his eyes, LORD, so that he may see." Then the LORD opened the servant's eyes, and he looked and saw the hills full of horses and chariots of fire all around Elisha.'

Many times, we can be so overwhelmed by circumstances: bills coming in, the problems and disasters that happen in the world. In these circumstances, weighing up the odds is the worldly way of looking at things. However, if we think of David in front of Goliath, Moses in front of the Red Sea, Jonah before Nineveh, Esther before the King. Time and time again men and women of God had the odds stacked against them.

In today's Scripture, it says, "Don't be afraid". How many times in scripture do we see the words "Don't be afraid"? Fear is one of the enemy's most used weapons. In the natural, the odds are almost always against us. If we walk by sight and not by faith, we will be crippled by fear. But if we allow the Lord to open our supernatural eyes, to see with the eyes of faith, we will always know, "Those who are with us are more than those who are with them."

Chris Tomlin's song, "*Our God is Greater*", says: 'Our God is greater, Our God is stronger, God you are higher than any other, Our God is healer awesome in power our God!'

Prayer

We need to proclaim those words no matter what the odds are, and like Jehoshaphat know that "The battle is not yours, but God's." Praise and worship your way through any battle!

Write your thoughts here, what is God saying to you about this passage?

DAY 81

Matthew 6:6 NIV

"'But when you pray, go into your room, close the door and pray to your Father, who is unseen. Then your Father, who sees what is done in secret, will reward you.'"

6 times in this chapter Matthew uses the 'R' word. He says to give, pray and fast. However, if they're done with a prideful heart, you've already received your reward. He's asking the question, are you doing these things as a show for others to see? Or are you doing them truly because you have your heart in the right place.

The promise is that you will receive a reward. Everyone wants a reward! There are rewards programs for everything today, but it doesn't matter what your heart is like. You can have any bad attitude, and you'll still be rewarded. However, God he looks to the heart. He is Spirit, and he looks at our spirit.

Our rewards can be either on earth, or in heaven. I love and welcome the rewards here; an abundant life on earth, but it's a great revelation to know we're storing up treasures in heaven. We'll spend a lot more time there, than here! Christianity has a great life insurance plan, the benefits are eternal, and out of this world!

Prayer

Father, I recommit myself to the basics, to prayer and ministry of the Word. I'm grateful for your reward program; it's by far the best one I've joined. Forgive me for chasing after worldly things. I will seek first your kingdom today! For yours is the kingdom, the power and the glory forever and ever. Amen.

Write your thoughts here, what is God saying to you about this passage?

DAY 82

Matthew 20:27-28 NIV

Whoever wants to become great among you must be your servant, and whoever wants to be first must be your slave — just as the Son of Man did not come to be served, but to serve and to give his life as a ransom for many.

We spend so much time improving our houses, and cars and material things that don't last, but what investment are we making in eternity. If we all truly realised how short our time is here on earth compared to eternity, we might live our lives differently!

The more we put our hand to the plow, the more we humble ourselves and obey the call on our lives, the more treasures in heaven, the jewels in our crown we receive.

John Bevere explains in his book, "*Honors Reward*," that you won't just be judged on what you did, but you will be judged on what you did in response to the call of God on your life. We can do lots of good things, but have we done the God things, the things God has called us too.?

Prayer

Father, thank you for sending your Son as a ransom for my life. I will serve you, with all my heart, for all my days. Give me your heart Lord for those I'm serving. Give me the mind of Christ. In Jesus' name, Amen.

Write your thoughts here, what is God saying to you about this passage?

Chapter 2

GOD SPOTS FOR RADIO

1. Research shows that the divorce rate for couples who marry in a church is 40%. For those married by a Celebrant it's 60%. For those who live together before they are married it's 80%. And for those couples who read their bible daily it's 1 in 1051 that get divorced. When we follow God's design of marriage, it's always the best way. The Bible tells us to seek Wisdom from God above all else. To forgive each other, to serve one another in love. This is the opposite to the world's way. The world says live for yourself, the Bible says to Love God & love others. With all the confusion and attacks on marriage. Maybe it's time we get back to a firm foundation, let's pray for stronger marriages, and for wisdom in our families.

2. Once there was a river that was infested with dangerous crocodiles. People from the nearby village would often be attacked and lose limbs and have terrible scars, and sometimes lives would be lost. But the longstanding tradition of the village was that people would never talk about the crocodiles, it was a taboo subject. Many people see the subject of Sex as a Taboo subject. They have a longstanding tradition that it is never talked about, and sadly many people are never properly educated on the subject. The Bible has lots to say about sex. We should be talking about it in our families, in our churches and in our relationships. Otherwise, people will believe what Hollywood & the media & the schoolyard believes. But God's way is always the best way.

3. Many people love the icing on the cake. I've even seen some kids just eat the icing and leave the cake on the plate. However, the way cakes are created, it's best to eat both, and too much icing is not good for you! Sex is a bit like the icing on the cake. You need the cake with all its flour & eggs and other goodies to make the cake, then the icing on the cake is the final topping. And it's not the key ingredient. In our relationships, we need to have lots of ingredients to make it successful, and sex is the icing on the cake, after the wedding. Sex has been designed by God for married couples, as a part of a healthy relationship, and in the marriage covenant. And God's way is always the best way.

4. According to the university of Iowa, the average two-year-old child hears 432 negative statements each day, but only 32 positive statements each day. And by the time your kid is in high school he or she will hear an average of 15 negative comments to every one

positive! The Bibles says in Ephesians 4:29, don't use any foul or abusive language. Let everything you say be good and helpful, so that your words will be an encouragement to those who hear them. Let's choose to speak life today and always look for an opportunity to build others up, not tear them down.

5. An old Chinese pastor once said, "There are 3 kinds of Christians. Some who have the bible but don't read it, they don't count. Some who read the bible & don't live it out, they don't count. And there are those who read the bible and live it out, those are the ones who count. We have a lot to learn from Chinese Christians, they have seen incredible revival in the midst of persecution. Another underground Chinese Pastor once said that their churches were raided, their bibles would often be burned by authorities, and their members were imprisoned or worse. But whenever they saw persecution, their underground church would grow. Maybe we should be a little more committed to studying God's word, and even if we are not persecuted, we should be getting to know the bible, and more importantly, getting to know the God of the bible. Maybe we'd see revival in ourselves, and then it could flow to those around us.

6. Brother Andrew from Open Doors, well known from the book, "God's Smuggler," took a courageous risk many years ago & started smuggling Bibles into Communist China. He prayed the now famous prayer, "Lord you can make blind eyes see, now make seeing eyes blind." The guards at the checkpoint didn't see the bibles in his little V dub beetle, and he started the first of many bibles smuggling missions. Open Doors now reaches out to many persecuted believers all over the world. What a History maker. From

one courageous risk, so many have been reached. They say that Leadership is not just what you accomplish, but what you set in motion. What can you do today to make history?

7. A little boy once said to his mum, "Who's book is this?" The mum replied, "It's God's book, the Bible." Then the boy said, "Well why don't we return it? We never read it?" Many in the West have several bibles in each house, we have them on apps, online, on cd, DVD and some may still listen in on cassette or video tape! The Purpose of God's Word is for teaching, rebuking, correcting & training in righteousness, so that every person will be thoroughly equipped for every work. 2 Timothy 3:16. Sadly, many are not taught, rebuked, corrected, or trained. We need to study God's word in private, for self-feeding, & in community for growth. Why don't you pick up God's book today?

Chapter 3

ARTICLES

DON'T WASTE A CRISIS

Some leadership lessons I've learned:

- Never waste a crisis, you can learn from every situation.
- Don't make big decisions on the spare of the moment.
- You will never please everybody, just try to do what is right.
- People show their true character when they are under pressure.
- Treat people with dignity & respect at all times.
- Be careful not to raise your voice or say things you will regret.
- Emails & text messages can be taken the wrong way, talk things through face to face if possible.
- You don't have to rush into anything.

- With Board issues, you don't have to tell your spouse everything, sometimes it's best to protect them.
- Don't be too idealistic, there will always be messes, don't have too high an expectation that everything will turn out perfect.
- Don't be prideful, always be willing to accept advice & admit your mistakes.
- Proverbs 19:20 NIV says, "Listen to advice and accept discipline, and at the end you will be counted among the wise." Find mentors who can be a sounding board, don't be afraid to ask for help.
- Take time off to reflect & rethink your direction if you can.
- Romans 8:28 NIV says, "And we know that in all things, God works for the good of those who love him, who have been called according to his purpose." God knows the end from the beginning, sometimes you can look back & see that God was moving the chess pieces around for his purposes.
- Pruning is good for growth, it hurts, but it makes a plant healthy.
- It's always good to have a witness.
- Carefronting is always a better option than confronting. Love is always the best option.
- Write a timeline of events so everyone is clear on what has transpired.
- When you aren't sleeping well, and you are running on empty, do whatever it takes to rest, otherwise you will be no good to anyone.
- Be careful not to take your stress out on your family, or the dog!
- Keep communication lines open, be on the front foot, otherwise people can jump to conclusions.
- Friendship is paramount, to work well with people. Healthy friendships are important, meeting together socially is important to build relationships.

- ❖ Don't blame everything on the devil, sometimes God is at work.
- ❖ Prayer is key, always pray privately & corporately.
- ❖ When you believe you have a prompting from the Lord, be very sure before you act on it. Sometimes people play the "God card," and they spiritualize things. I do believe God speaks to us, some people believe He speaks to us about every little detail of our lives, some believe He rarely speaks to us & that he gave us a brain, wisdom, discernment & a conscience to work things out with the tools he's already given us. Either way, if we say, "God told us", and he didn't tell us, we are misrepresenting God. We must be cautious in this area. 1 Thessalonians 5:16-22 NIV says, "Rejoice always, pray continually, give thanks in all circumstances; for this is God's will for you in Christ Jesus. Do not quench the Spirit. Do not treat prophecies with contempt but test them all; hold on to what is good, 22 reject every kind of evil."
- ❖ Choose your words wisely, whatever you say, remember it could be repeated & could come back to bite you
- ❖ Always care for the sheep. Sheep have a different perspective than shepherds
- ❖ Look at situations from the top of the tree. If you are in the jungle, you will only see the trees around you. Rise up & look ahead.
- ❖ A wise chess player can see 7 moves ahead before he makes his next move. Consider the flow on effects of every move you make.
- ❖ Always be looking at what leaders you can raise up.
- ❖ When a church goes to a new level, it must change the way its leaders relate to the people. In a small church, the leaders are normally available to everyone, as it grows, they will be less available.

Why you should be in ministry

I believe there are many people who are called to "Full-time ministry," who haven't yet taken the step of faith to fulfil their destiny. There is a stigma about being a Pastor that people think it's only for the special chosen ones, or the ones with that "higher calling" that is so high that not many will ever reach that height.

Let me clear up some misconceptions first. I do believe every Christian is called to "Full-time ministry." Wherever we are in life all Christians are called to minister to people. In our marriages, our homes, our workplace, in the sports arena, on holidays, etc. Wherever we are we should be ambassadors for Christ.

I believe everyone in churches should be serving and using their spiritual gifts to build up the church. It is wrong thinking to assume that the ones with ministry titles should be the ones doing ministry, while everyone else is a spectator. We are all called to participate and serve wherever we are planted.

However, I've felt the need to write this article because I believe there is a crisis in the Body of Christ. I believe many are called to leave their secular jobs and be trained and equipped to serve full-time working for a church or a parachurch ministry. But many people haven't, or won't step out in ministry because of fear, or they are following a shadow mission, or they just haven't been asked…

I remember at the age of 17, chatting with my Youth Pastor. I told him I wanted to go to Bible College and go straight into ministry after completion. He suggested that I should get a job in the secular marketplace for a season first. It was great advice! I did go to Bible College, but then I spent a number of years selling advertising at radio stations, building relationships with business people, learning the ropes of the way the corporate world worked. It was a great training ground! But then I felt a calling to lay it down and step into youth ministry. I was earning good money in my career! I remember the scripture that came to me, "Those who do not take up their cross and follow in my steps are not fit to be my disciples. 39 Those who try to gain their own life will lose it; but those who lose their life for my sake will gain it." Matthew 10:38-39 (Good News Translation). Think about the disciples and the price they had to pay. They had to give up their fishing businesses, their tax collecting business and so forth. Regardless of their professions, eleven of the disciples immediately left behind everything to follow Jesus.

There is a price to pay. Financially, it doesn't look like a smart decision in the world's eyes. But do we truly trust in the Lord to provide our every need? The truth is, one day we will all stand before God and be judged for the works we have done on this earth. As Christians, we know we are saved by faith, not by works. But we are saved to do something. Ephesians 2:10 NIV says, 'For we are God's handiwork, created in Christ Jesus to do good works, which God prepared in advance for us to do.'

Some are called to work in the secular marketplace and to shine a light in that arena. Colossians 3:23-24 ESV says, "Whatever you do, work heartily, as for the Lord and not for men, knowing that from the Lord you will receive the inheritance as your reward. You are serving the Lord Christ." But if you are called to quit your job and serve in Church ministry, then I challenge you to make your move! I have spoken to many people over the years, and I've thought, "That person would make a great pastor!" Sometimes I've challenged the person, sometimes I've kept it to myself. But I feel I need to speak out and throw out this challenge to anyone reading this.

Some people have this cookie-cutter view of a pastor. Thinking they have to fit into a certain mould. Some people look at mega church pastors and think they have to measure up to that image. Mega churches make up less than one percent of Christians around the world. God Bless them! They do a great work! But research shows that in smaller churches, more people use their spiritual gifts more, whereas many attendees at mega churches just attend, and don't use their gifts. At Bible College I remember reading, "Church Planting for a greater harvest," by C Peter Wagner. It outlined that church planting is the most effective way to evangelise and change the spiritual atmosphere of a community. We need more Church Planters and more churches and more pastors to reach the world for a great last day's harvest!

Now the term "Pastor," is the main title we use in evangelical churches. It's a cultural thing, and people put all sorts of religious expectations on Pastors. The truth is every person called to ministry has unique gifts and callings. We should never compare one pastor to another. Some are more gifted at teaching, or evangelism, or healing or the prophetic. After many years of pastoring, I Learnt to be comfortable in my own skin, and be myself, and to function in my stronger gifts and to be content with who I'm called to be. "Comparison is the thief of joy." We must avoid the trap of trying to be someone else!

I was inspired to hear that after Billy Graham preached in Australia in 1959, that the next few years, the Bible colleges were filled with people training for the ministry. I know many Pastors who are in ministry now because of his ministry. I know a number of Pastors who were inspired to be in ministry because of Clark Taylor, Trevor Chandler, Phil Pringle, Brian Houston, and others. Another friend of mine once told me he knows of 28 people who are now pastors because he had challenged them and raised them up in ministry. I remember Trevor Chandler once saying, "Leadership isn't just what you achieve, but what you set in motion." We need to raise up the next generation of leaders. I feel the need to focus my life on raising up more leaders, the same way that great leaders have believed in me and given me a chance.

At my current stage in life, I want to keep doing the work of the ministry, but I also see the crucial importance of raising up other leaders. And not just young people! Some churches write people off if they are over a certain age. Now I do believe we need to raise up young leaders, but as C.S. Lewis said, "You are never too old to set another goal or to dream a new dream." Smith Wigglesworth was in his late 40's when he launched into ministry. I think one of the beautiful things about the Body of Christ is that young and old, black, or white, male, or female, we are all called to work together in unity, shoulder to shoulder. 1 Corinthians 3:6-9 NIV says, "I planted the seed, Apollos watered it, but God has been making it grow. So neither the one who plants nor the one who waters is anything, but only God, who makes things grow. The one who plants and the one who waters have one purpose, and they will each be rewarded according to their own labour. For we are co-workers in God's service; you are God's field, God's building."

I worked as a youth Pastor for 10 years and was Bi-vocational. I always had a number of jobs on the side to bring in an income. Then when I was 30 and my wife Carol and I had been married a few years, I was working in Christian Radio Sales, earning good money! I felt the Lord call me to do "an evangelistic work in the city." That was the call. It wasn't any more detailed. Some people are waiting for a vision from heaven with a name, a place, a date, and a cosy income with the exact amount of money needed to cover your bases! So, Carol and I prayed together, and through a series of "God-incidences," we joined New Hope Church Brisbane. It was a half hour drive from where we were living. We were very happy at Pine Rivers Vineyard church. Carol had been there for 15 years, and I'd been there for 3 years. We were both serving in ministry. I was Treasurer of the board, preaching occasionally, and Carol was helping run Alpha and Creche. When we told our Pastors that we felt called to New Hope, they gracefully blessed us. They even announced it at church and laid hands on us and prayed for us for our new step of faith. I've seen many people leave churches for the wrong reasons. We were very reluctant and hesitant to leave our church, but we received many confirmations and we made sure it was of God before we left. Little did we know what was to come…

After joining New Hope and adjusting to life with our newborn boy Joshua, we started to get more involved at New Hope. I was invited to preach on the first Sunday in January, I was given the text of the Parable of the Sower. And I remember the Lord stirring my heart that we all need to sow the word of God like a seed. But then I got a revelation from the final verse in that parable, "But the seed falling on good soil refers to someone who hears the word and understands it. This is the one who produces a crop, yielding a hundred, sixty or thirty times what was sown," Matthew 13:23 NIV. We are all called to produce a crop. I knew God had planted me in this church to produce a crop.

Soon after I was invited to a "Doing Church as a Team," conference at New Hope Hawaii. It changed my life! I was so inspired by Pastor Wayne Cordeiro, his teaching about doing daily devotions, about having a servant heart, and that the whole church is a team that works towards souls being saved. It was so refreshing! On the first night of the conference, Pastor Phil McCallum, Founding Pastor of New Hope Brisbane, took me out for coffee. He shared with me that God was calling him back to Hawaii to work with Pastor Wayne, and he asked me to pray about becoming Senior Pastor of New Hope Brisbane. I was so shocked! It was a moment when my life flashed before my eyes, and I felt that everything in my life was preparation for this moment. I remember Phil said something along the lines of "The local church is the hope of the world. There is nothing more important than to serve in the local church."

I remember thinking that it was nice to be asked, but that it would never really work. I was too young, too inexperienced, not trained enough. I was a divorcee that was re-married. I was a Coffs Harbour boy, living in the big city. I was better off staying in radio and playing it safe. That is just what the devil wanted me to think! Play it safe! Don't step out of your comfort zone, don't rock the boat! What will your family say? What if everyone leaves the church? Who wants to listen to me preach, I haven't got anything to say?

The truth is I was unqualified. I was too young. I wasn't the prefect person for the job… But God. God doesn't call the equipped, he equips the called! I remembered the verse from 1 Timothy 4:12-14 NIV, "Don't let anyone look down on you because you are young, but set an example for the believers in speech, in conduct, in love, in faith and in purity. Until I come, devote yourself to the public reading of Scripture, to preaching and to teaching. Do not neglect your gift, which was given you through prophecy when the body of elders laid their hands on you." What a powerful verse. DO NOT NEGLECT YOUR GIFT! We will be held accountable one day for the gifts that have been given to us. Luke 12:48 ESV says, "Everyone to whom much was given, of him much will be required…"

I called my wife from Hawaii and told her I'd been offered the role. She said, "Come home! You've got conference fever! We've just had a baby! Come back and help me change nappies!" She wasn't really into the idea at first. But then she prayed about it. And we spoke to her mum when I was back. She wisely said, "You'd better know that God has called you. Without God's calling you won't succeed." So, we pressed into God to seek him about our calling. Carol heard a sermon from Brian Houston that inspired her. He said, imagine being at a footy game and not barracking for either team. It would be pretty boring! You've got to pick a team, and then be all in!" The same with our Christian faith. We've got to be passionately, all in for Jesus! This really spoke to Carol, and it helped her make up her mind to follow this calling.

I remember hearing two songs that inspired me at the time. One was from Caedmon's Call's song "*Thankful*". It said, "I say that I'm so thankful that I'm incapable of doing' any good on my own." This reminded me that it was only in God's strength that I could live a life worthy of the calling.

And the other song was "*Voice of Truth*," from Casting Crowns:

"Oh what I would do to have
The kind of faith it takes
To climb out of this boat I'm in
Onto the crashing waves
To step out of my comfort zone
Into the realm of the unknown where Jesus is
And He's holding out His hand

But the waves are calling out my name
And they laugh at me
Reminding me of all the times I've tried before and failed
The waves they keep on telling me
Time and time again. "Boy, you'll never win!"

"You'll never win!"
But the Voice of Truth tells me a different story
The Voice of Truth says, "Do not be afraid!"
And the Voice of Truth says, "This is for My glory"
Out of all the voices calling out to me
I will choose to listen and believe the Voice of Truth."

There are many voices telling us we can't do it. But God's voice is the only one that matters. So, we took the leap of faith. It was way out of our comfort zone! We had a 4 month transition where Pastor Phil took me under his wing and mentored and trained me. I was working bi-vocationally at the time. The church couldn't afford to pay me at the time, so I threw out a fleece and the Lord provided a job at a local home loan company. I was paid a full-time wage to work part-time as business development manager and part-time as Associate Pastor. Thankfully this continued for several months until the church was out of debt and could afford to pay me full-time. What a miracle of provision!

I really want to honour my wife Carol. When we married, she knew I loved the Lord, but she didn't know I'd become a Pastor. It was a massive change for her to become a Pastor's wife, while raising little children. She made many sacrifices and had to put up with so much rubbish over the years. But we believe in "One-flesh" ministry. When one is called the other is also. And she has been a rock alongside me through thick and thin, in sickness and in health! She is now a very confident preacher, she has run the children's ministry for many years, she's looked after the church administration team, and she's held the fort down while I've been away. She's had her heart broken many times when people close to us have moved on. And she's stood firm with the call of God on her life, no matter what storms have come our way.

Many people from her past were surprised when they found out she and her husband had become Pastors. But just like me, I believe all the events of her life had prepared her for the role God has called her to. No-one knows the amount of hard work and the hours she's poured into people's lives over the years. She will be richly rewarded for the sacrifices she has made. She's only paid two days a week but works about eight days a week for the kingdom! Often I'm the one that gets the pat on the back for doing what we do. But she is the unsung hero who I know will have so many jewels in her crown in heaven for her faithfulness.

This is what it comes down to: faithfulness. Will you be found faithful with what God has called you to do? Another song that has spurred me on is called "Faithful One" from David Ruis:

"The narrow pathway
Through the needle's eye
I'm stepping forward
To the place I die

For I know that You are faithful
As we walk these fields of white

To the waiting and the humble
Your Kingdom comes

The way of mercy
Takes me to the least
Down the road of suffering
To the wedding feast

For I know that
You are faithful
As we walk these fields of white
To the weary and the hurting
Your Kingdom comes"

Are you willing to die to your own agenda and plans and fully surrender yourself to the Lord? Some people reading this will think this is directed at them. I have had several people on my heart as I've been writing this. And I often wonder if the model Jesus used should be the way we should do ministry. Find twelve men, and teach them everything you know, and commission them to ministry. I started a ministry school at New Hope in the second half of 2019. And I feel like this was one of the most important things I did in ministry. In the past we have had interns serving in the church, this is something I believe we should be intentional about and make available to those who want to step up.

Some people might not be sure of their calling. Nothing ventured, nothing gained! Norman Vincent Peale said, '*Shoot for the moon even if you miss you'll land among the stars.*' Just like the Aussie saying, "Have a go ya mug!" Step out in faith, if it's God's will, it will bear fruit, if not, then I'm sure another door will open. What have you got to lose? If you do step out in ministry, then potentially, souls will be saved from a Christless eternity, marriages will be strengthened, lives will be transformed, the poor will be cared for, who knows what can be accomplished? If you don't step out in ministry, you will keep getting the fruit you are seeing in your life.

I remember a preacher once saying whatever is your holy discontent is probably what your called to. If you can't stand people going to hell, you're an evangelist, if you can't stand seeing people with no Bible knowledge, you're called to the teaching ministry. Romans 12:6-8 NIV says, "In his grace, God has given us different gifts for doing certain things well. So if God has given you the ability to prophesy, speak out with as much faith as God has given you. If your gift is serving others, serve them well. If you are a teacher, teach well. If your gift is to encourage others, be encouraging. If it is giving, give generously. If God has given you leadership ability, take the responsibility seriously. And if you have a gift for showing kindness to others, do it gladly." Find your gifting and calling and step out!

1 Corinthians 15:58 NIV says, "Always give yourselves fully to the work of the Lord, because you know that your labour in the Lord is not in vain." I used to be frustrated when I had to work for secular companies and do ministry on the side. I just wanted to preach and minister full-time. I know it was an important season for me, but then the Lord opened doors for me. Is the Lord opening doors for you? Will you be obedient and walk through them?

Serving in full-time in ministry doesn't have to be in a church. It can be in a Parachurch organisation, in Christian Media, as a chaplain, as a missionary, at a Rehab. You could start a new ministry! They say that many of the jobs that will be available in the workforce in the future, haven't even been invented yet! Think about how social media, Uber, Air BnB many of these companies didn't exist years ago, and now millions are employed worldwide. Don't put ministry in a box. God may have something in store for you that you've never heard of before! So, I encourage you to get trained, get equipped, be available. God isn't looking for ability, he's looking for availability.

I took one of our young guys from New Hope Church on an 8 day mission trip a few years ago. We preached 14 times and saw over 150 people come to Christ. Along the way, we prayed, we worshipped, we spoke about the things of God. I was able to speak into his life. I felt the Lord challenge me that I need to raise up many more people in ministry, and that this is a great model. He then got inspired and organised a trip back to India to his hometown to preach. He preached several times and saw about 150 people get saved! This is the way the kingdom works. Spiritual mothers and Fathers, raising up spiritual sons and daughters, and kicking them out of the nest! It's the principle of multiplication!

I heard Francis Chan make the statement recently, "*A disciple isn't really a disciple until they are discipling someone else.*" It's the best way to grow in our faith! When we have to minister to other people, we have to feed ourselves, so we have something to feed others!

Just like Paul would take Timothy on trips, and then Paul would send Timothy on trips. Just like Jesus had John, James, and Peter and the 12, the 72, he would send them out. Ephesians 4:11-12 says, "So Christ himself gave the apostles, the prophets, the evangelists, the pastors and teachers, to equip his people for works of service, so that the body of Christ may be built up." We are called to equip HIS people for works of service.

John Wesley said, "Give me one hundred preachers who fear nothing but sin and desire nothing but God, and I care not a straw whether they be clergymen or laymen, such alone will shake the gates of hell and set up the kingdom of heaven on earth."

Matt Prater

Dad Jokes & other tidbits...

I like to tell Dad jokes... *sometimes he laughs!*

What kind of car did the disciples drive? *A Honda, because they were all in one Accord!*

How does Jesus like his steak? *Well Done good & Faithful servant, well Done!*

Why is Christianity the most dramatic religion? *Because other religions are do, do, do... but Christianity is done, done, done!*

Did you know that Jesus is divine? *And we are de branches.*

Why doesn't Jesus wear Jewellery? *Because he breaks every chain!*

Who is the best financier in the Bible? *Noah. He was floating his stock while the rest of the world was in liquidation!*

What are you if you believe in God but only 12.5%? *An eighth theist!*

Who was the most business savvy woman in the Bible? *Pharaohs daughter, she went to the bank of the Nile and drew out a little prophet!*

Satan is depicted as a snake in the Bible because a snake has no arms or legs. That means the devil has been... *Dis-armed, and De-feeted!*

Did you know that Rick Warren wrote a book for dolphins? *It's called the Porpoise Driven Life!*

What did Adam say the on the night before Christmas? *"It's Christmas, Eve."*

Why didn't the Lions eat Daniel? *They were on a Daniel Fast!*

Christian pick-up lines:

How would you like to join my Purpose Driven Life?

Hi! I've been reading the book of Number lately, and I was wondering can I have yours?

Did you say your name was Esther? Oh, I guess I just think you were chosen for such a time as this.

Hi. My name is Will... God's Will.

I put the stud in Bible study.

I would fight for you… like the 3rd monkey on the ramp of the Ark!

Is your name Grace? Because you are amazing.

So… do you pray here often?

Why are there fences around cemeteries? People are dying to get in…

Cemeteries: The dead centre of town…

I saw 2 guys walking around the cemetery for ages, when I asked them what was wrong, they said they've lost the plot!

The good thing about funeral directors is they'll be the last ones to let you down!

My friend was given a coffin as a gift, he said, This will be the last thing I need!

I saw a sign for a funeral company on the highway that said, Please slow down… we don't want to see you for a very long time!

What's wrong, Bill? asked the pastor. I need you to pray for my hearing, said Bill. The pastor put his hands on Bill's ears and prayed. When he was done, he asked, So how's your hearing? I don't know, said Bill. It's at the courthouse on Monday!

A pastor is speaking to his church. He tells them, 'I have good and bad news. The good news is, we have enough money to pay off all the church debts and build a new wing to the church.' The congregation clapped and cheered. He continues. 'The bad news is, it's still in your pockets.'

… as Pastor Smith is about to deliver his sermon he asks the congregation how many of them managed to read Mark Chapter 17 as he'd asked them to the previous Sunday. Almost all hands in the church went up. "Very well," Pastor Smith continued. "By the way, Mark only has 16 chapters, and the topic of today's sermon shall be lying."

The Sheep on the fringe – A Poem by Matt Prater

> To the sheep on the fringe who feel rejected & alone, you are welcome to come to a place that feels like home,
>
> to the broken & the wounded you can come & find love, to the hurting & the struggling, come & get help from above,
>
> If you stay on the fringe it's where the sheep get attacked, so walk closer to the shepherd, he's always got your back,
>
> He will comfort & calm you, he will heal & restore, just walk closer to the shepherd, not on the fringe any more,
>
> Come, lay down your burdens, find rest for your soul, stop running away, the good shepherd can make you whole.

Here's some of Matt's favourite quotes:

- "If you do what you've always done you'll get what you've always got"
- "The Main thing is to keep the main thing the main thing".
- "There's 2 ways you can wake up in the morning. You can say 'Good Lord, it's morning!' or 'good morning, Lord!' – I recommend the latter".
- "Let Prayer be your steering wheel not your spare wheel".
- "God likes people with big ears more than big mouths".
- "Revival runs in rivers not canals".

- "God loves availability more than ability".
- "It's one thing to get an answer to prayer but another thing to be an answer to prayer".
- "One good turn gets all the bedsheets".
- "Don't say look what the world is coming too, say look Who's come to the world"!
- "God doesn't call the equipped, he equips the called"

Here's a few great Bible verses:

Jeremiah 29:11-14

For I know the Plans I have for you declares the Lord plans to prosper you and not to harm you plans to give you a hope and a future. Then you will call upon me and come and pray to me, and I will listen to you. You will seek me and find me when you seek me with all of your heart. I will be found by you declares the Lord.

John 3:16 – For God so loved the world that he gave his one and only Son, that whoever believes in him will not perish but have eternal life.

Ephesians 2:8-9

For by grace you have been saved through faith. And this is not your own doing; it is the gift of God, not a result of works, so that no one may boast.

Titus 3:5

He saved us, not because of works done by us in righteousness, but according to his own mercy, by the washing of regeneration and renewal of the Holy Spirit

Romans 10:9

Because, if you confess with your mouth that Jesus is Lord and believe in your heart that God raised him from the dead, you will be saved.

Acts 4:12

And there is salvation in no one else, for there is no other name under heaven given among men by which we must be saved.

John 14:6

Jesus said to him, "I am the way, and the truth, and the life. No one comes to the Father except through me."

Acts 16:30-33

Then he brought them out and said, "Sirs, what must I do to be saved?" And they said, "Believe in the Lord Jesus, and you will be saved, you and your household." And they spoke the word of the Lord to him and to all who were in his house. And he took them the same hour of the night and washed their wounds; and he was baptized at once, he and all his family.

Thanks for reading my book! Mark Twain said, "The two most important days in your life are the day you are born and the day you find out why." I believe every one of us was created to have a relationship with God through his Son Jesus Christ. If you would like to get your heart right with God & come to Christ I'd love to talk with you more! Some people think they have sinned too much & that God won't accept them. But you don't clean yourself before you get in the shower, you get in the shower to get clean! In the same way, we all need to come to Christ with our sins, and he will wash us whiter than snow!

If you want to pray to receive Jesus as Lord & Saviour, pray this prayer to start your relationship with God:

Father God in Heaven, thank you for sending Jesus, to die on the Cross for me. Lord, I admit I am a sinner. I need and want Your forgiveness. I accept Your death as the penalty for my sin, and recognize that Your mercy and grace is a gift You offer to me because of Your great love, not based on anything I have done. Cleanse me and make me Your child. By faith I receive You into my heart as the Son of God and as Saviour and Lord of my life. From now on, help me live for You. Please filled me with your Holy Spirit! In Jesus name, Amen.

My advice is to pray every day, Read the Bible daily, join a Church, and tell others about Jesus!

Please email me if you have prayed that prayer, and we will send you more info about following Jesus. info@historymakersradio.com